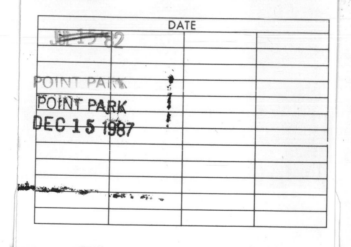

BERTRAND
RUSSELL
AND HIS WORLD

RONALD CLARK

BERTRAND RUSSELL
AND HIS WORLD

with 105 illustrations

THAMES AND HUDSON

Frontispiece: Bertrand Russell in 1960.

ACKNOWLEDGMENTS

The author and publishers would like to thank Kenneth Blackwell, of the Bertrand Russell Archives, McMaster University, Ontario, and Professor John Slater, of Toronto University, for their help in the preparation of this book.

© 1981 Ronald Clark
First published in the USA in 1981 by Thames and Hudson, Inc., 500 Fifth Avenue, New York, New York 10110
Library of Congress Catalog Card Number 81-50617

Printed and bound in Great Britain by William Clowes (Beccles) Limited, Beccles and London.

A studio portrait of Bertrand Russell taken by Hugh Cecil, probably about 1913.

ANGUISH OFTEN CLARIFIES THE MIND. Thus Bertrand Russell's clear thought and exposition, leading from one point to the next through the thickets of mathematics, philosophy and morals, may have owed much to the frequent agonies of his life when intellectual problems appeared insoluble, emotional troubles seemed unresolvable, and suicide beckoned invitingly. At times he was kept going only by the aristocratic duty to lead in which he believed so strongly.

His identification with a small group whose virtues he saw as 'fearlessness, independence of judgment, emancipation from the herd, and leisurely culture' provided strength and comfort throughout much of his long life. In Lady Ottoline Morrell, the most famous of his mistresses, he found a 'kind of restfulness and sense of home-coming' when he 'came in contact with [her] aristocratic habits of mind'. And at the age of 92 he confessed that his ideal period was France in the 1780s. 'I should like to have been a French aristocrat shortly before the storming of the Bastille', he added. 'Eighteenth-century rationalism was delightful and humane. Oppression was real but not sufficiently severe to prevent inspired rebellion from the thinkers of the time.' As his daughter has said, 'To him, as to most Russells, privilege meant obligation, the duty to provide for others the benefits he himself enjoyed.'

With this obligation went an assessment of human capacity which would today lay him open to the charge of elitism, that gravest of contemporary sins. As a young man he could write: 'Surely one Darwin is more important than 30 million working men and women.' And, a few years later: 'What can a charwoman know of the spirits of great men or the records of falling empires or the haunting visions of art and reason? Let us not delude ourselves with the hope that the

Russell's parents, Lord and Lady Amberley, in the study of their home at Ravenscroft, Trelleck, in October 1871, seven months before he was born. *Above right:* A drawing of Russell made by Lady Amberley. She died when he was aged two, and the sketch must have been made shortly before this. Along the side she wrote: 'Bertrand's favourite attitude for study – book resting on feet.'

best is within the reach of all.' Many of his later verdicts on education were on modern lines, but he could still write: 'A great deal of needless pain and friction would be saved to clever children if they were not compelled to associate intimately with stupid contemporaries.' And during old age his controversial but at times percipient secretary Ralph Schoenman could say of the serious intellectual doubts which inhibited Russell from engaging wholeheartedly in mass movements with revolutionary aims: 'He felt that cultural excellence and unique achievement were the product of favoured circumstances.'

The belief in a duty to lead, whatever the consequences, had brought dangers as well as rewards to Russell's father, Lord Amberley, son of the 1st Earl Russell. Within a few years of marrying Kate, daughter of the 2nd Lord Stanley of Alderley, Amberley's support for birth-control had wrecked his chances of success in the general election of 1868 and brought to an end his brief foray into public life. Disillusioned, he retired to the country and quietly devoted the rest of his short life to the philosophical *Analysis of Religious Belief.*

The Amberleys' home, Ravenscroft, was a long low-built eighteenth-century house standing above the lower Wye Valley in South Wales. Here Bertrand Arthur William Russell was born on 18 May 1872, younger brother to John Francis Stanley, always known as Frank, eight years older than himself, and to an infant sister Rachel.

The Queen, whom Russell was to meet as a child during one of her visits to his grandparents, was little more than half way through her

Above: Russell's birthplace, depicted in a contemporary watercolour. 'Shortly before I was born', he wrote, '[my parents] went to live in a very lonely house called Ravenscroft (now called Cleddan Hall) in a wood just above the steep banks of the Wye.' *Left:* Russell's parents, with his brother Frank and sister Rachel, outside the front door of Ravenscroft. Standing in the doorway are Lizzie Williams, the wet nurse who stayed on as a servant after Frank's birth, and her husband.

reign. The German Empire had, it is true, been re-established the previous year following the end of the Franco-Prussian War. In Geneva a court of arbitration was about to find Britain legally responsible for the depredations of the *Alabama* and other Confederate cruisers during the American Civil War. Wilhelm Wundt's *Physiological Psychology* and James Clerk Maxwell's *A Treatise on Electricity and Magnetism*, both to produce their own revolutions in thought, were already in the press, while Darwin's *The Descent of Man*, published the previous year, continued to be the subject for fervent debate. Yet in spite of these faintly worrying events it was difficult to realize that the Victorian age would not last for ever, that its imperial ideas, supported where necessary by the ingenious new Gatling gun, would not continue to spread. Despite the family weakness for new beliefs which had removed Amberley from the public scene, it appeared that his younger son, like the rest of the Russells, was destined for a secure place in a secure world.

Misfortune, which was to dog Russell's footsteps so frequently, arrived quickly. In May, 1874 Frank was struck down by diphtheria. Russell and his sister Rachel were packed off to Pembroke Lodge, their grandparents' home in Richmond Park on the outskirts of London. Frank recovered after intensive nursing by his mother. Little was known in those days about the contagious period of diphtheria and the other children were brought home too soon. Rachel caught the disease and Lady Amberley, still exhausted from nursing Frank, felt obliged to provide the same care for her daughter; she caught the infection and died three days later. Her daughter died five days after her mother. Lord Amberley, who recorded that his 'two greatest treasures in this world are gone almost at one blow', grew steadily weak from grief. He died early in 1876, technically the victim of bronchitis, but apparently from the lack of any will to live.

The sudden loss of mother, father and sister would have been sufficiently traumatic for any small boy. The events were to be quickly compounded by what followed. Russell's free-thinking parents had appointed two atheists as guardians, to take over after their deaths. One was Thomas James Cobden-Sanderson, book-binder, printer and founder of the Doves Press; the second was D. A. Spalding, a young scientist earlier employed as a tutor for Frank. The prospects of the two Russell boys being brought up by two atheists might just have been stomached by their grandparents, Lord and Lady John Russell. But Amberley's papers revealed that Lady Amberley had, in Bertrand Russell's words, 'allowed [the tubercular Spalding] to live with her, although I know of no evidence that she derived any pleasure from doing so'. The two guardians, warned by counsel that in the circumstances they would have no chance of defending their guardianship in court, quietly capitulated. In February 1876 Russell was delivered to Pembroke Lodge, Richmond Park, the home of his paternal grandparents and two of their surviving children, Agatha and Rollo.

Russell in 1876, the year in which his father died. His mother had died two years previously and he was now sent to live with his grandparents, Lord and Lady Russell, in Pembroke Lodge, Richmond Park.

Above: Pembroke Lodge. Queen Victoria visited the Lodge in 1874 when Russell, aged two, was staying there. 'Bertie', reported his Aunt Agatha, 'made a nice little bow – but he was much subdued and did not treat Her Majesty with the utter disrespect I expected.' *Right:* Lord John Russell, Bertrand's grandfather and one of the most important of Victorian Prime Ministers. He died in 1878, aged 86, two years after Russell was brought to live at Pembroke Lodge. *Far right:* His grandmother, under whose stern care he spent most of his youth.

Opposite: Bertrand with his Aunt Agatha, who also lived at Pembroke Lodge throughout the whole of Bertrand's youth.

A family group outside the summer house of Pembroke Lodge, 1863, showing (left to right): Dr Wagner, tutor to Lord Amberley's brother and sister; William Russell (BR's uncle); Lady Russell; Rollo Russell (BR's uncle); Georgy, daughter of Lord John by his first wife; Lord Amberley; Lord Russell; Agatha Russell (BR's aunt).

The child who had lost the easy-going environment of Ravenscroft was now poured into the straitjacket of a life which toughened him physically and intellectually, starved him emotionally and, more than any other factor, made him the man he was to become. The surroundings of Pembroke Lodge, which looked out on to the wilds of Richmond Park and backed on to a panoramic view of the Thames and the Surrey hills, offered to a small boy almost as much adventure as the Ravenscroft estate. But life in the new home had an unhealthy closeness to the remote past. Russell's maternal grandmother had taken tea regularly in Florence with the widow of Bonnie Prince Charlie, the Young Pretender. And Lord John, who was 84 when Russell came into his care, had visited Napoleon on Elba and attended the Congress of Vienna that had settled the frontiers of nineteenth-century Europe. 'I lived wholly in the past', Russell was to write of his years at Pembroke Lodge. '[Lady Russell] would call me by mistake by the names of people who were dead.' There were other side-effects of living in a home whose master, taken for bath-chair tours of the grounds, had twice been Queen Victoria's Prime Minister, and had held a multiplicity of other Cabinet posts. When other men spoke of the government as 'they', Bertrand Russell often said 'we'.

The spartan regime of Pembroke Lodge which, all the year round, started with a cold bath and half an hour's piano practice before family prayers at eight, was good training for the rigours of the outer world. What it lacked was contact with the rough-and-tumble of life that a public school might have provided. But when the time came, Lady Russell had no wish to repeat her experiences with brother Frank, a young man who attracted trouble as a magnet attracts iron filings. Frank had been sent to Winchester, with results which can be gathered from the comment of George Santayana: 'Bertie at least must be preserved pure, religious, and affectionate; he must be fitted to take his grandfather's place as Prime Minister and continue the sacred work of Reform.' So Bertie, after a few terms at a local kindergarten, was handed over to a succession of governesses and tutors.

At Pembroke Lodge, where Lord John died in 1878, Russell was left, as he put it, 'to loneliness and reserve'. Diary entries and a private journal written in Greek characters and disguised as Greek exercises, provide contemporary evidence of much misery. In later life he at times looked back through tinted spectacles, recollecting in his autobiography: 'My childhood was, on the whole, happy and straightforward, and I felt affection for most of the grown ups with whom I was brought into contact.' But in memoirs never written for publication he admitted: 'From adolescence onwards I was driven by

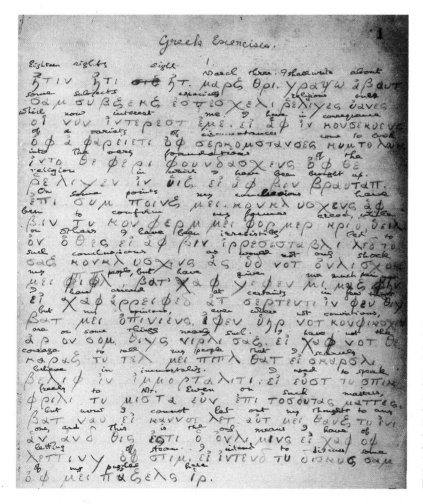

A page from the private journal, written in Greek characters and disguised as Greek exercises, in which Russell recorded his personal feelings. This entry, dated 3 March 1888, starts: 'I shall write about some subjects, especially religious ones, which now interest me. I have in consequence of a variety of circumstances come to look into the very foundations of the religion in which I have been brought up.'

a desperate misery of loneliness for which I knew that love would be the only cure.'

With the loneliness there went an equally desperate desire for certainty, for intellectual reassurance that can easily be seen in Freudian terms as reaction to his transfer from mother to granny and governesses, from a happy family environment to a life where duty rather than love was the requirement of the day. Thus the stern tradition of Lady Russell may have led to more than she can have expected. For it was the unsatisfied desire for certainty as a boy that was to guide his future.

The first indication came when his brother Frank was teaching him the elements of Euclid. Russell was later to write:

> This was one of the great events of my life, as dazzling as first love. I had not imagined that there was anything so delicious in the world. . . . I had been told that Euclid proved, and was much disappointed that he started with axioms. At first I refused to accept them unless my brother could offer some reason for doing so, but he said: 'If you do not accept them we cannot go on', and as I wished to go on, I reluctantly admitted them *pro tem*. The doubt as to the premises of mathematics which I felt at that moment remained with me, and determined the course of my subsequent work.

Love, if not certainty, was eventually to come, and at an early age. Uncle Rollo, Lord Amberley's brother, was to provide the introduction. In 1883 the Rt. Hon. Rollo Russell married, left the Pembroke Lodge household, and set up home in a house on the slopes of Hindhead, the sandy prow of hills forty miles west of London. Nearby lived John Tyndall, scientist and mountaineer, who aroused Russell's ambitions to become a physicist, abandoned only when he realized that 'laboratories & experiments & mechanisms [baffled him] completely'. Nearby there also lived the Pearsall Smiths, a family of rich Philadelphia Quakers who had settled into the Friday's Hill estate, a few miles from Uncle Rollo.

The Pearsall Smiths were show-piece Americans. The father, Robert, was the flourishing head of a glass-blowing firm and a popular evangelist until either indiscretion or bad luck made him less acceptable among the select groups of spinsters who were his main followers. His wife Hannah, moved equally by dormant sadism and religious fervour, had written *The Christian's Secret of Happy Life* which had sold more than a quarter of a million copies. His son was Logan, eventually to become a notable *littérateur*. His elder daughter, Mary, was, after a first marriage, to become the wife of Bernard Berenson; his younger, Alys, was in 1894 to becomes Alys Russell.

Uncle Rollo, an unaware *deus ex machina* out for an afternoon stroll, decided to introduce his nephew to the Americans. The Pearsall Smiths fell in love with Russell; Russell fell in love with Alys.

He was only 17 and for some while his grandmother continued to be more concerned with his education than with any unfortunate

Alys Pearsall Smith, Russell's first wife, in 1897. She once told her sister Mary: 'Thee can get on relying on thy charm, but I have got to be good.'

15

results of contact with American Quakers. Mathematics appeared to be the one subject for which he showed marked ability and enthusiasm, and it was for a mathematical scholarship to Trinity College, Cambridge, that he sat in December 1889.

The subject had already drawn him for two reasons. One was the almost mystic quality with which he endowed it. The second was that mathematics was not human and had 'nothing particular to do with this planet or with the whole accidental universe – because, like Spinoza's God, it won't love us in return'.

Examined by Alfred North Whitehead, later to become his collaborator and friend, Russell won his scholarship and in October 1890 began an undergraduate life which for the first time brought him into close contact with a society wider than that offered by Pembroke Lodge. He was elected to the Apostles, a very small society which prided itself on electing the most promising undergraduates to membership. He formed close friendships with G. E. Moore, and with the three great-nephews of Macaulay, Charles, Robert and George Trevelyan. A good deal of the earnestness he had breathed in under granny's tutelage was dissolved in a happy university life.

Left: Russell as a Trinity College undergraduate in 1891. *Right:* G. E. Moore, a friend of Russell's undergraduate days, seen in 1925 when he was University Lecturer in Moral Science at Cambridge.

A group of Russell's friends at Trinity, showing Charles Trevelyan (far right, centre row), later Master of Trinity, and (left and centre, top row) Crompton Llewelyn Davies and Theodore Llewelyn Davies.

At the end of three years he was bracketed Seventh Wrangler in the Mathematical Tripos. But just as religious doubt was already shredding Lady Russell's comforting Christianity, so did the work entailed in the Tripos raise doubts about the foundations of mathematics. 'The attempt to acquire examination technique had led me to think of mathematics as consisting of artful dodges and ingenious devices and as altogether too much like a crossword puzzle', he wrote. What he wanted to restore his faith in mathematics was 'some reason for supposing [it] true'. He turned to philosophy.

In the Cambridge of the 1890s, philosophy was still dominated by the Absolute Idealists, who followed Hegel's belief that ultimate reality consists of mind, or spirit, rather than matter. Russell had tended to accept this during his first three years at Trinity, but it was only during his fourth year that he entered the Idealist camp without reservations. 'There was', he has written, 'a curious pleasure in making oneself believe that time and space are unreal, that matter is an illusion, and that the world really consists of nothing but mind.'

Holding these views, he sat for the Moral Science Tripos in the summer of 1894 and gained an honours degree, a happy event which Lady Russell saw as prelude to a parliamentary or academic career, the first years of which would naturally be spent under her sheltering wing. Russell had other ideas.

His coming-of-age in 1893 had brought with it a £20,000 legacy from Lord Amberley's estate, and once the Tripos was out of the way he proposed to Alys. The engagement was considered cautiously at

Right: Hannah Pearsall Smith and her husband Robert, the parents of Russell's first wife Alys, playing a card game in the garden of their Friday's Hill home in 1894, the year in which their daughter married Russell.

Below: The Marquess of Dufferin and Ava, British Ambassador in Paris, to whom Russell was appointed attaché for three months in 1894. The Marquess had been attaché to Lord John Russell at the close of the Crimean War. A portrait by B. Constant.

Friday's Hill by a family not yet certain what the Hon. Bertrand Arthur William Russell would make of himself as a husband. At Pembroke Lodge the news was received with horror, since the addition to the family of a Quaker, five years older than Russell, daughter of an American manufacturer, looked like the end of the world.

Lady Russell was quickly at action stations. First, through the family doctor, Russell was told that Uncle Willy, comfortingly described as ill, was in fact mad. Aunt Agatha had broken off an engagement following insane delusions. There were other examples of lunatics in the family and Russell now began to consider the house where he had been brought up as 'a family vault haunted by the ghosts of maniacs'.

However, to combat the fear that he and Alys might add to the family list of those who had to be put away, there was one answer: they would have no children. The suggestion further scandalized

Lady Russell, who now capitalized on her health, invoked the distress that would be caused by her grandson's proposed marriage, and drew from him a promise not to see his beloved for three months. To strengthen her position, she called in the aid of Lord Dufferin and Ava, attaché to the late Lord John almost half a century before. Now the British Ambassador in Paris, he was persuaded to appoint Russell as his temporary attaché in that city. To Lady Russell it must have seemed impossible that the prim attractions of an American Quaker would not be swamped by the more sophisticated allurements of Paris.

Russell dutifully spent his three months in Paris and kept his promise not to see Alys; even when he returned across the channel for a long weekend in Cambridge to address the Apostles, he merely sent her a letter. Travelling back to Paris, he had as companion Mary Costelloe, Alys's sister, now leaving her husband and *en route* to join Bernard Berenson whom she was eventually to marry. She and Russell stayed in adjoining apartments at the Hotel Vouillemont, went to the Opera together, exchanged kisses and, in Russell's words, talked 'about sexual morality & my reasons for preferring chastity to vice'. In old age he was to tell close friends of an 'affaire' with Mary and any reader of his letters to Alys back in England, including a confession which he headed 'A Psychological Explanation', might conclude that it was a sexual affaire. Yet this seems unlikely, although from early youth Russell was attractive to women in a way not easily explained. His height of 5 ft. 9 in. was barely average, he was slight of build and with hair that quickly went grey. His hazel eyes, like his intellect, regarded most things sceptically and in purely physical terms it was only in old age, when anger with injustice filled him with the wrath of God, that he presented a commanding figure. The two

Far left: Alys Pearsall Smith. A *carte de visite* portrait of Russell's first wife, recently discovered in his undergraduate wallet. *Left:* Mary Pearsall Smith, sister of Russell's first wife Alys. She amiably accepted Russell's falling out of love with her sister and wrote to him of 'continuing friendliness and good wishes'.

Alys Pearsall Smith in her
Quaker wedding dress,
13 December 1894.

qualities which transformed him were energy and self-confidence. Genetically he had been lucky and the stern regime of Pembroke Lodge had built on the luck so that after a hard day debating or teaching, cycling or walking, he remained as bright as the proverbial new pin; as for self-confidence, it was surely agreed that the Russells were born to show the world the way it should go.

Russell returned from Paris with love for Alys undiminished and they were married in a Quaker ceremony on 13 December 1894. Thus he cut himself off, not from home in its cosy sense, but at least from an environment in which he had lived for nearly two decades. Half a century later, when Pembroke Lodge had been taken over by the Civil Service, he was to write: 'Almost every night before falling asleep I see the garden in which I passed my childhood, which has since been destroyed; I mind its destruction quite as much as the deaths of people I have loved.' But in 1894 he had already given it up.

Early in 1895 Russell and his wife set off for a tour of the Continent. They spent three months in Berlin, crossed the Alps to Fiesole where Mary Costelloe had settled in a villa close to Bernard Berenson, continued with a leisurely progress down the Adriatic from Ravenna to Ancona, and in early summer returned to England. Here they set up home in a small cottage at Fernhurst, two miles from the Pearsall Smiths at Friday's Hill.

In near-idyllic surroundings, Russell now considered what he would do for a living. There was, of course, no need to do anything. Quite apart from the financial safety-net of the Pearsall Smiths, his own income was sufficient, if not for expensive living at least for the contemplative kind of life which attracted him. In Berlin he had considered devoting himself to two contrasting varieties of work. He would write 'a series of books in the philosophy of the sciences, growing gradually more concrete as I passed from mathematics to biology'; and he would 'also write a series of books on social and political questions, growing gradually more abstract'. He was to carry out his early resolution more faithfully than he may have foreseen at the time. For the next three-quarters of a century his writings, both academic and popular, were regularly to switch from one field to the other, then back again. The result was that no other Englishman of the twentieth century was to gain such high regard in both academic and non-academic worlds.

This dichotomy of interests was first illustrated during the latter half of 1895. At Fernhurst Russell began 'An Essay on the Foundations of Geometry', his thesis for a Trinity Prize Fellowship, awarded annually for members writing on a subject of their own choice. In October he learned that he had been awarded the fellowship, and a few weeks later left for Berlin once again with Alys, intent now on studying the workings and potential influence of the German Social Democratic Party.

Above: Fiesole, near where Bernard Berenson and Russell's sister-in-law settled in I Tatti. Among the olive groves and cypresses covering the surrounding hills Russell wrote 'A Free Man's Worship'.

Left: Alys Russell outside the door of Millhanger, Fernhurst, a sixteenth-century workman's cottage where, in 1895, Russell settled down to the study of mathematics.

GERMAN SOCIAL DEMOCRACY

SIX LECTURES

BY

BERTRAND RUSSELL, B.A.

FELLOW OF TRINITY COLLEGE, CAMBRIDGE

WITH AN APPENDIX

ON SOCIAL DEMOCRACY AND THE WOMAN
QUESTION IN GERMANY

BY ALYS RUSSELL, B.A.

LONGMANS, GREEN, AND CO.
LONDON, NEW YORK, AND BOMBAY
1896

The title-page of Russell's first book, written following research with his wife in Berlin.

Russell's essay, providing his own answer to the question 'How is Geometry Possible?', was based on the thesis that all space had a constant measure of curvature – an idea that was, as he later admitted, swept away in 1916 by Einstein. 'The geometry in [his] General Theory of Relativity is such as I had declared to be impossible. The theory of tensors, upon which Einstein based himself, would have been useful to me, but I never heard of it until he used it.' Yet the six-year fellowship gave him a status which was increased when, on the Russells' return from their second visit to Berlin, he gave six lectures on German Social Democracy at the newly-formed London School of Economics, and lectured on the same subject to the Fabian Society. Printed as a book, the material brought praise from *The Times* for 'knowledge and lucidity', 'fair-minded spirit' and 'insight and judgment'.

German Social Democracy was the first example of Russell's ability to research a subject speedily and then distil his research in fluent prose that any educated man could understand. That ability, which largely accounted for the great influence which he exercised for something like three-quarters of a century, was to be demonstrated in books, booklets, learned papers and popular articles which ranged far beyond philosophy, mathematics and politics. The rights of women and the future of technology, the problems of education and the morals of war were among the more serious subjects with which he dealt. But he wrote just as persuasively on 'Love and Money', 'On the Fierceness of Vegetarians' and 'Should Socialists Smoke Good Cigars?'

In the autumn of 1896 the Russells visited the United States. At the women's college of Bryn Mawr, where Alys had been educated – and whose President, Dr Carey Thomas, was her cousin – and at Johns Hopkins University in Baltimore, Russell lectured on the foundations of geometry. After a social visit to Harvard they returned to England and settled into Millhanger, a new home on the outskirts of Fernhurst. Here Russell began seriously on the first major task he had set himself: the building of a new structure of mathematics which would enable the simplest laws of logic, and the most abstruse theorems of advanced mathematics, to be developed from a small number of primitive ideas. If it could be done, then none of the accepted axioms and concepts need be assumed, and logic and mathematics would form a single system of truths.

During this period Russell started to doubt his Idealistic beliefs. It was indeed inevitable if he were ever to satisfy himself about the objective truth of mathematics, since the Idealists believed that all rested in the mind of the beholder, while Russell's aim was to prove mathematics independent of the mathematicians.

'Moore led the way', he was to write years later, 'but I followed closely in his footsteps.' He was hurried along the path by preparation of a series of lectures on Leibniz in 1899, later published as *A Critical Exposition of the Philosophy of Leibniz*. It convinced him that he must

struggle from what he now saw as the Idealistic morass. Eventually the process was complete.

I felt it, in fact, as a great liberation, as if I had escaped from a hot-house on to a wind-swept headland. I hated the stuffiness involved in supposing that space and time were only in my mind. I liked the starry heavens even better than the moral law, and could not bear Kant's view that the one I liked best was only a subjective figment. In the first exuberance of liberation, I became a naïve realist and rejoiced in the thought that grass is really green, in spite of the adverse opinion of all philosophers from Locke onwards.

Russell's construction of a new logical foundation for mathematics was carried out between the last few years of the nineteenth century and 1909, first in *The Principles of Mathematics*, published in 1903, and then in *Principia Mathematica*, written jointly by Russell and Whitehead and published in three volumes between 1910 and 1913.

This concentrated intellectual work, the most considerable of Russell's achievements, was carried out against a background of emotional chaos, and it would be unrealistic to believe that one did not influence the other, even had the characters involved in the intellectual and emotional dramas not been the same.

Early in 1901 Russell underwent a traumatic experience on seeing Mrs Whitehead in acute pain; a year later he realized that he was no longer in love with Alys. The evidence that the two events were linked, and that Russell had in fact fallen in love with Mrs Whitehead, is circumstantial but considerable, including a personal

Bryn Mawr College, Pennsylvania, where Russell in 1896 gave a course of lectures based on his Fellowship Thesis, soon to be published as *An Essay on the Foundations of Geometry*. President of the College was the formidable Dr Carey Thomas, a cousin of Russell's wife, Alys.

diary which Russell kept at the time and numerous later letters to Lady Ottoline Morrell, his mistress for a number of years. How much Evelyn Whitehead knew of Russell's feelings for her – 'Much my strongest affection after my love for you', he wrote to Ottoline, 'is my affection for Mrs Whitehead' – remains unknown. On Mrs Whitehead's instructions, all Russell's letters to her were burned after her death.

In his autobiography he relates how in February 1901 he and Alys returned to the house in Cambridge where they were staying with the Whiteheads. Mrs Whitehead was in great pain, apparently from a heart attack, and Russell realized with desperate suddenness what his feelings were. In his own words, it was a 'conversion'; he became intensely aware of the human predicament, moved towards pacifism, and soon afterwards 'turned to all ways of alleviating [Mrs Whitehead's] trouble without seeming to know it'. Part at least of the trouble was Whitehead's improvidence, and over the next few years Russell surreptitiously filtered money into the Whitehead household through Evelyn Whitehead.

Almost exactly a year after the 'conversion' Russell, lecturing at Trinity for a couple of terms following the end of his Prize Fellowship, realized that he no longer loved Alys. Significantly enough, they were staying at Mill House, Grantchester, the Whiteheads' new home a few miles from Cambridge. The revelation came, according to Russell, on an afternoon bicycle ride. 'I had had no idea until this moment that my love for her was even lessening', he later claimed. 'The problem presented by this discovery was very grave.' He was

Mill House, Grantchester, Alfred North Whitehead's home during the early years of the twentieth century, when he and Russell were together writing *Principia Mathematica*.

unable to conceal from Alys the fact that he no longer loved her, and from 1902 until their parting in 1911 they endured together a life of mutual misery; but at least it drove Russell to an even more desperate concentration on mathematics.

The agonizing experience was to produce one of his most famous essays, 'A Free Man's Worship', much of it written in Bernard Berenson's house, I Tatti, where the Russells spent the Christmas of 1902. Mary Costelloe had married Berenson after Frank Costelloe's death and the couple were ecstatically happy. Russell, as distraught as Alys by the fact that love had vanished, walked upon the cypress-covered hills behind the house, and sublimated his unhappiness into the short essay, 'the total result of so much suffering', as he described it. A cry of despair, it was uttered in such lyrical prose that its attractions lasted long after the author had begun to qualify what he had written.

By this time, he had gone some way towards satisfying himself on the truth of mathematics. There were, towards the end of the nineteenth century, two contrasting views on the nature of mathematical propositions. Mill and his followers had seen them as empirical generalizations, supported by what appeared to be an almost infinite number of examples; the Kantian view was that they

The Villa I Tatti in the first decade of the twentieth century.

were synthetic *a priori* truths. Neither analysis satisfied Russell, who since his later days at Cambridge had hoped to show that mathematical propositions could be derived from the propositions of formal logic.

Before it could be done, two steps had to be taken. First, the fundamental concepts of mathematics had to be defined in logical terms; secondly, a system of logic had to be developed which was comprehensive enough to allow every mathematical proposition to be deduced from it. On the Continent the first problem had been tackled by both Gottlob Frege and Giuseppe Peano, but their work was comparatively little known in England and it was only after meeting Peano in Paris that Russell felt confident enough to start completing what he called 'the big book'.

His visit to Paris was made with Alys and the Whiteheads to attend the International Congress of Philosophy, Logic and the History of Science. 'In discussions at the Congress', Russell later wrote, 'I observed that [Peano] was always more precise than anyone else, and that he invariably got the better of any argument upon which he embarked. As the days went by, I decided that this must be owing to his mathematical logic.' He approached Peano, was given a set of the Italian's off-prints and returned to England much delighted.

Russell spent two months studying and extending Peano's system; re-drafted what he had written and then carried on with the book. Much of the work was done at Millhanger, some of it in the Whiteheads' Mill House where Whitehead was writing the second volume of his *Universal Algebra*. Its character is shown by a progress report to Uncle Rollo:

> I did one of the hardest days of work that I have done ever in my life: seven hours real work, and two correcting proofs from Peano. I had the hardest Chapter of my book to write, and I was anxious to finish it within the day, while my mind was full of the subject. I succeeded, tho' it was thirty pages, but once or twice I found myself forgetting everything in heaven and earth, as I did during my Tripos. I have been so long without real work, that I have come back to it with a kind of fever: *everything* else seems unreal and shadowy to me just now and I work as if I were possessed. If only I can keep it up, I shall get a great deal done.

Eventually, the 200,000-word draft was completed. There followed six months of further revision and then, without warning, the discovery of what has become known as the Russell paradox. There had been mathematical examples of the paradox – a statement which is true if, and only if, it is also false – before Russell, but the best-known were typified by the non-mathematical conundrum of Epimenides the Cretan who stated that all Cretans were liars. As Russell was to write, no one took such paradoxes seriously until, towards the end of the nineteenth century, they were seen to bear on important mathematical problems.

Then there came his disturbing discovery. As he has explained it:

Cantor had a proof that there is no greatest number, and it seemed to me that the number of all the things in the world ought to be the greatest possible. Accordingly I examined his proof with some minuteness, and endeavoured to apply it to the class of all the things there are. This led me to consider those classes which are not members of themselves, and to ask whether the class of such classes is or is not a member of itself. I found that either answer implies its contradictory.

However he studied the matter he could see no easy way out of the problem. Whitehead responded on hearing the news with 'never glad confident morning again'. Eventually, Russell worked out a temporary and crude way round the paradox and handed the manuscript to the publishers.

But that was the beginning rather than the end of the paradox problem. He now realized that Frege had used as an axiom of constructing his classes, or sets, the very method which led to the paradox. Frege, told of the situation, expressed consternation. Russell now provided additional explanations of 'The Contradiction' and, when proofs of his book began to arrive, deleted whole pages. Finally, he added two appendices. One described Frege's views and the other described a first rough method of dealing with the paradox. Not everyone was satisfied. Henri Poincaré, who had little sympathy with the new logic, remarked that 'formal logic is not barren, it brings forth contradictions'.

Russell's immersion in the deeps of mathematics is revealed in a letter to Gilbert Murray. 'I created with all an artist's passion for the perfect, a new treatment of Symbolic Logic', he said of *The Principles of Mathematics*, 'and to my joy Whitehead finds that it has all the beauty and perfection that I hoped.'

Gilbert Murray, who married one of Russell's cousins, Lady Mary Howard, and at the turn of the century settled at Churt, a few miles from the Russell home in Fernhurst. Russell's early friendship with Murray was disrupted by their differing views on the First World War.

Long before *The Principles of Mathematics* had secured Russell a place in the academic hierarchy, he and Whitehead had decided to join forces in preparing 'a complete investigation of the foundations of every branch of mathematical thought'. Russell was about to start on volume two of *The Principles* which would have proved that all mathematics followed from the logical principles of his first volume; Whitehead was already at work on the second volume of his *Universal Algebra*, his attempt to discover the common principles of the various algebras to be found in logic and mathematics. 'We . . . discovered that our projected volumes were practically on identical topics', Whitehead later recorded, 'so we coalesced to produce a joint work. We hoped that a short period of one year or so would complete the job. Then our horizon extended and, in the course of eight or nine years, *Principia Mathematica* was produced.'

The enterprise, 'one of the great intellectual monuments of all time', was carried on with an heroic determination and an almost mystic passion. 'Dear Bertie', wrote Whitehead at the top of one page of equations, 'The following seems to me rather beautiful.' To Russell, what made the work vital and fruitful was 'the absolute unbridled Titanic passion that I have put into it. It is passion that has made my intellect clear, passion that has made me never stop to ask myself if the work was worth doing, passion that has made me not care if no human being ever read a word of it. . . .'

The philosophical aspect was largely handled by Russell, the mathematical by Whitehead; but every section, once written, was then scrutinized by the other collaborator and amended, then read and, if necessary, amended once again by the original writer. Hardly one of the 2,000 pages, Russell said later, could be attributed entirely to either of them.

Before the project had got seriously under way Russell had moved from Millhanger. The emotional break with Alys had been the start of a period during which they both wanted as few reminders as possible of the home in which they had lived after their marriage. They rented houses in London, and in Surrey, but had found it impossible to settle in any of them. Then, after two years, Russell determined to make a new start and commissioned an old Trinity friend to design a house at Bagley Wood, on the southern outskirts of Oxford. The site was no doubt chosen out of consideration for Alys. Her brother Logan had a few years earlier bought Court Place, a fine house on the Thames below Oxford, and her widowed mother had joined her son there. The new home was only a few miles away.

Here Russell began to see a way through the obscurities of the contradiction. And he also began to see his way to the solution of another problem which impeded his and Whitehead's grand design. The latter problem led to the discovery of his Theory of Descriptions which he often mentioned as his key single contribution to philosophy.

It was first given to the world in 'On Denoting', and is best described in Russell's later words. After pointing out that statements

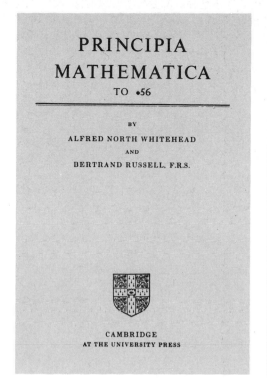

PRINCIPIA
MATHEMATICA
TO *56

BY

ALFRED NORTH WHITEHEAD

AND

BERTRAND RUSSELL, F.R.S.

CAMBRIDGE
AT THE UNIVERSITY PRESS

about, for instance, 'the golden mountain', could misleadingly attribute to it some sort of existence, he pointed out that according to his theory when a statement containing a phrase of the form 'the so-and-so' was rightly analysed, then that phrase would disappear. He went on:

> For example, take the statement 'Scott was the author of *Waverley*.' The theory interprets this statement as saying: 'One and only one man wrote *Waverley*, and that man was Scott.' Or more fully: 'There is an entity c such that the statement "x wrote *Waverley*" is true if x is c and false otherwise; moreover c is Scott.'
>
> The first part of this, before the word 'moreover', is defined as meaning: 'The author of *Waverley* exists (or existed or will exist).' Thus 'The golden mountain does not exist' means: 'There is no entity c such that "x is golden and mountainous" is true when x is c, but not otherwise.'

Thus, he concludes, the puzzle as to what is meant by the statement, 'The golden mountain does not exist', disappears.

The Theory of Descriptions was first published in *Mind*; his answer to the problem of the contradiction was given in 'Mathematical Logic as based on the Theory of Types' in the *American Journal of Mathematics*. The Theory of Types provides for a lowest level which consists of individuals, a next higher level which consists of classes of individuals, a next higher level which consists of classes of classes of individuals, and so on. The theory also stipulates that only a member

Above left: The title-page of the first volume of *Principia Mathematica*. The Royal Society subsidized publication, but the two authors still had to provide £100. *Above:* Alfred North Whitehead had been the Trinity examiner who recommended Russell for a mathematical scholarship in 1889. For years a friend and co-worker with Russell, he disagreed with him about the First World War. The earlier friendship was never totally restored.

of the immediately lower level can be a member of a class at a given level. Thus it makes it impossible for a class to include itself as a member, and thereby solves the contradiction. This was a refined form of the solution which Russell had included as an appendix to *The Principles of Mathematics*.

The physical problems of work on *Principia Mathematica* were increased by the fact that even in their final form the thousands of pages had to be written out in longhand; the symbolic logic included such devices as a 'U' on its side for 'implies', a curving bar for 'not', a three-barred equals sign for 'is equivalent to' and other symbols that were not carried on any typewriter.

Before the task was completed, Russell was elected to the Royal Society on the strength of 'his researches concerning the Principles of Mathematics and the Mathematical Treatment of the Logic of Relations'. Proposal apparently depended, he wrote shortly afterwards, 'upon the chance of some big-wig taking one up', and in his case the big-wig was Whitehead, himself elected a Fellow five years earlier. In mid-May, 1908, he travelled to London from Bagley Wood to be admitted. It was a typically full day. First he did an hour and a half's work on *Principia*. In the train he read proofs of the French edition of his book on Leibniz and then attended a meeting of the Women's Suffrage Committee. Following the Royal Society proceedings he arrived home at 8.00 p.m., wrote an article, several letters on Women's Suffrage, and critical comments on a book he had been reading in manuscript, probably Graham Wallas's *Human Nature in Politics*. He was still hard at work on *Principia* with, he estimated, between 4,000 and 6,000 manuscript pages to go. 'I have no time to think about anything, which is very pleasant', he concluded, 'and it is comforting to have a big continuous job on hand.'

Not until the following summer was Whitehead, announcing that he was to see the Cambridge University Press, able to write: 'Land in sight at last.' And not until October 1909 was the manuscript finally delivered. But on the final lap of the course there had been a disappointment. The publishers were willing to subsidize the printing to the tune of £300. It had been hoped that the Royal Society would provide the further £300 that the Press expected to lose on the publication. But the Society obliged with only £200 and the authors paid the rest from their own pockets. 'We thus earned minus £50 each by ten years' work', Russell observed. 'This beats the record of *Paradise Lost*.'

From Russell's own words it might be thought that for more than a decade the problems of mathematics and logic filled even the nooks and crannies of his mind. This was not so. While at Cambridge he had for long taken it for granted that he would enter politics, an idea which he gave up only when the attractions of mathematics became too strong. But political interest had remained. He had been a founder-member of Sidney Webb's 'Co-efficients', started to discuss the problems of Empire, and had resigned only when it became too

*8·343. $\vdash :. (\exists x) . \phi x . \supset . q : \supset : \{(\exists x) . \chi x\} \mid q . \supset . \{(\exists x) . \phi x\} \mid \{(\exists x) . \chi x\}$

Prefix to matrix is $(y, z, u, v, y', z', u', v') : (\exists a, x, x')$.

Call the matrix $\qquad\qquad f(a, x, x')$.

It is true if $\qquad\qquad \sim\chi z . \sim\chi v . \sim\chi z' . \sim\chi v' \qquad\qquad$ (1)

Also $\qquad\qquad \chi z . q . \supset . f(a, z, z) . \supset . (\exists a, x, x') . f(a, x, x') \qquad$ (2)

Similarly if we have $\qquad \chi v . q$ or $\chi z' . q$ or $\chi v' . q \qquad\qquad$ (3)

From (1).(2).(3), by *8·28, $q . \supset . (\exists a, x, x') . f(a, x, x') \qquad$ (4)

Now $\phi a . \sim q . \supset . f(a, x, x')$. Hence

$$\phi y . \sim q . \supset . f(y, x, x') . \supset . (\exists a, x, x') . f(a, x, x')$$

Similarly for $\phi z . \sim q$, $\phi y' . \sim q$, $\phi z' . \sim q$. Hence

$$\phi y \vee \phi z \vee \phi y' \vee \phi z' . \sim q . \supset . (\exists a, x, x') . f(a, x, x') \qquad (5)$$

But $\qquad\qquad \sim\phi y . \sim\phi z . \sim\phi y' . \sim\phi z' . \supset . f(a, x, x') \qquad\qquad$ (6)

By (5) and (6), $\qquad \sim q . \supset . (\exists a, x, x') . f(a, x, x') \qquad\qquad$ (7)

$\vdash . (4) . (7) . \text{*8·28} . \supset \vdash . \text{Prop}$

In the next four propositions, q and r are replaced by propositions containing apparent variables, while p remains elementary.

*8·35. $\vdash :. p . \supset . (x) . \psi x : \supset : \{(x) . \chi x\} \mid \{(x) . \psi x\} . \supset . p \mid \{(x) . \chi x\}$

Putting $q . = . (x) . \psi x$, $s . = . (x) . \psi x$, the proposition is

$$(p \mid \sim q) \mid \sim \{(s \mid q) \mid \sim (p \mid s)\}.$$

We have by the definitions

$$\sim q . = . (\exists b, c) . \psi b \mid \psi c,$$
$$p \mid \sim q . = . (b, c) . p \mid (\psi b \mid \psi c),$$
$$s \mid q . = . (\exists x, y) . \chi y \mid \psi x,$$
$$p \mid s . = . (\exists z) . p \mid \chi z,$$
$$\sim (p \mid s) . = . (z, w) . (p \mid \chi z) \mid (p \mid \chi w),$$
$$(s \mid q) \mid \sim (p \mid s) . = : (x, y) : (\exists z, w) . (\chi y \mid \psi x) \mid \{(p \mid \chi z) \mid (p \mid \chi w)\}.$$

Put $\qquad f(x, y, z, w) . = . (\chi y \mid \psi x) \mid \{(p \mid \chi z) \mid (p \mid \chi w)\}.$

Then $\quad \sim \{(s \mid q) \mid \sim (p \mid s)\} . = : (\exists x, y, x', y') : (z, w, z', w') . f(x, y, z, w) \mid f(x', y', z', w'),$

$(p \mid \sim q) \mid \sim \{(s \mid q) \mid \sim (p \mid s)\} . = : (x, y, x', y') : (\exists b, c, z, w, z', w') .$
$\qquad\qquad\qquad\qquad\qquad\qquad \{p \mid (\psi b \mid \psi c)\} \mid \{f(x, y, z, w) \mid f(x', y', z', w')\}.$

Writing $\theta \hat{x}$ for $\sim\chi\hat{x}$, the matrix is equivalent to

$$p . \supset . \psi b . \psi c : \supset :. \psi x \supset \theta y . \supset : p . \supset . \theta z . \theta w :. \psi x' \supset \theta y' . \supset : p . \supset . \theta z' . \theta w'.$$

This is satisfied by putting $b = x . c = x' . z = w = y . z' = w' = y'$. Hence Prop. The same matrix appears in the next three propositions; only the prefix changes.

*8·351. $\vdash :. p . \supset . (x) . \psi x : \supset : \{(\exists x) . \chi x\} \mid \{(x) . \psi x\} . \supset . p \mid \{(\exists x) . \chi x\}$

Same matrix as in *8·35, but prefix $(x, z, w, x', z', w') : (\exists b, c, y, y')$.

Matrix is true if $\qquad\qquad \theta z . \theta w . \theta z' . \theta w'.$

Assume $\sim \theta z$, and put $y = y' = z . b = x . c = x'.$

A page from *Principia Mathematica*. 'I like mathematics', Russell wrote, 'because it is *not* human & has nothing particular to do with this planet or with the whole accidental universe – because, like Spinoza's God, it won't love us in return.'

right-wing for his tastes. He spoke occasionally in defence of Free Trade and served on the committee of the National Union of Women's Suffrage Societies. But he had written in 1903 that his second volume of *The Principles of Mathematics* totally absorbed him. When it was finished, he said, he would be too old and too inelastic to acquire the habits of a practical life. 'So politics is really out of the question.' *Principia* no doubt confirmed the view.

It was against this background that he decided to stand for Parliament in 1907; or, was persuaded to stand by the National

Marchers in Hyde Park on their way to a Votes for Women rally on 21 June 1908. Russell was a supporter of the National Union of Women's Suffrage Societies, for whom he stood – unsuccessfully – as a candidate in the Wimbledon by-election of 1907.

Union of Women's Suffrage Societies. He had been a keen supporter of women's rights even before coming under the influence of Alys; indeed, his belief that 'any improvement in the condition of the great mass of women is only possible through Socialism' was, he once said, the 'discovery which has made me a Socialist'. In 1907 the Wimbledon seat in south-west London had become vacant following the resignation of the Conservative MP. In his place there now stood Henry Chaplin, a formidable parliamentarian who had held a Lincolnshire seat for nearly forty years before being swept away in the Liberal landslide of 1906. The Liberals did not contest the seat but less than a month before polling day the National Union decided to enter a candidate. They 'think it desirable to run someone as a means of propaganda, & tho' I hate it, I can see no adequate reason to refuse, as no one else can be got at such short notice', Russell wrote to an acquaintance. 'I should of course in addition profess all my usual opinions. I should not do it if there was a chance of getting in, as I am determined not to go into politics. . . . It is a howling joke, & amuses me almost as much as it annoys me. . . .'

Nearly three-quarters of a century later it is difficult to see the significance of the 'howling joke'. But in the world of 1907 there was

THE NORTH AMERICAN
FOUNDED IN 1771.
The Oldest Daily Newspaper in America.
Descendant of the
Weekly Pennsylvania Gazette,
Founded by Benjamin Franklin in 1728.
Issued Every Day in the Year.
Published by
THE NORTH AMERICAN CO.
THE NORTH AMERICAN BUILDING
BROAD AND SANSOM STREETS
PHILADELPHIA

FRIDAY, MAY 3.

MRS. BERTRAND RUSSELL

Prominent as a woman suffrage leader in England, she is interested in trying to have her husband elected to Parliament. Mrs. Russell is a daughter of Mr. and Mrs. Robert Pearsall Smith, of Philadelphia, and her husband is the heir of his brother, Earl Russell.

ENGLISH SUFFRAGISTS FIGHT FOE'S ELECTION

Women Enter Campaign for Bertrand Russell, Philadelphian's Husband.

CHAPLIN GETS SURPRISE

LONDON, May 2

Woman suffragists have decided to oppose the election to the House of Commons of Henry Chaplin, ex-president of the local government board, who has been opposing equal suffrage.

He is the Unionist candidate for the vacancy at Wimbledon, caused by the resignation of Charles E. Hambro, Conservative.

Liberals are not contesting the seat, and Mr. Chaplin thought he had a walk-over; but today he was confronted by an active woman suffragist campaign in behalf of Bertrand Russell, brother and heir presumptive of Earl Russell.

Mr. Russell's wife, a daughter of Robert Pearsall Smith, of Philadelphia, has been closely identified with women's political work.

NORTH EAST SURREY (OR WIMBLEDON) DIVISION PARLIAMENTARY BYE ELECTION

Photo by the London Stereoscopic & Photographic Co. Ltd.
Regent Street, London W.

Alys Russell supported her husband's political campaign in the Wimbledon by-election of 1907. *Left: The North American* reports on Russell's unexpected decision. *Above:* An election pamphlet issued by Russell for the 1907 campaign. 'When in later years I campaigned against the First World War', he said, 'the popular opposition I encountered was not comparable to that which the suffragists met in 1907.'

something almost laughable about a candidate whose main plank was the demand that women should have the vote. The subject, as Russell later said, was treated with 'mere hilarity'. It was 'the comic side of the election' which according to the *Daily News* appealed to the electorate, and although Chaplin's electioneering concentrated on tariff reform and colonial preference, he could not resist remarking on 'that little band of masculine women and feminine men' opposing him.

Alys ably supported Russell in what was generally considered to be a freak election. Rats were let loose during his first public meeting and Alys was hit in the face by a thrown egg – an incident for which Chaplin apologized. There were few signs that many of the electorate found it possible to think seriously about an idea that might even lead to the unthinkable – women in Parliament. Against Chaplin's 10,263 votes, Russell mustered 3,299, some 4,000 less than the Liberals in the previous year's election.

The Wimbledon election introduced Russell to the hurly-burly of the market place, a useful 'blooding' for the future. It also provided a diversion from the misery of life at Bagley Wood, which was now resumed and which grew even more depressing when the great task of finishing the *Principia* came to an end.

Within the next two years this unsatisfactory life, during which Russell's suicidal tendencies were kept under control only by dislike of leaving his beloved mathematics, was to be transformed. While he was publicly to date the transformation from 1911, there are strong hints in his private correspondence that it began in September 1909, after a meeting with Philip Morrell, the MP for South Oxfordshire, and his wife Lady Ottoline, half-sister of the 6th Duke of Portland.

As an undergraduate, Russell had met Ottoline Morrell casually and had been remembered by her as that 'little mathematical wonder'. The acquaintance was renewed when Alys's brother Logan campaigned for Philip Morrell in the 1906 election which produced such a disastrous result for the Conservatives. Morrell was one of the 377 Liberals who had a majority of 84 over all other parties. In September 1909 Logan, living nearby with the widowed Mrs Pearsall Smith, drove the Morrells through the Oxfordshire lanes to meet his sister and brother-in-law.

'Ottoline', Russell later wrote, 'was very tall, with a long thin face something like a horse, and very beautiful hair of an unusual colour, more or less like that of marmalade, but rather darker.' 'Bertrand Russell is most fascinating', Ottoline wrote in her diary on the evening of that September meeting. 'I don't think I have ever met anyone more attractive, but very alarming, so quick and clear-sighted, and supremely intellectual – cutting false and real asunder. Somebody called him "The Day of Judgment".' In subsequent reminiscence Russell admitted that he also had been strongly affected by the meeting.

Augustus John's portrait of Lady Ottoline Morrell. Russell's affair with her, which began in 1911, transformed his life. Their friendship lasted until her death in 1938.

A few weeks later he finally delivered the manuscript of *Principia Mathematica* and, as he says, found himself at a loose end. At first his thoughts turned to politics, mainly, he has stated, because of his interest in the developing battle between the Commons and the Lords; he applied to Liberal headquarters for a constituency, and was recommended to Bedford. However, the admission that he was an agnostic ruled him out, 'a lucky escape' as he has called it, since while the Bedford Liberals were making up their minds he received an invitation from Trinity. Whitehead had decided to resign from his senior lectureship in mathematics and move to London. But he had proposed that the College should set up a lectureship in logic and the principles of mathematics so that the ideas presented in *Principia Mathematica* should continue to be taught there. Russell, the obvious choice, accepted the five-year appointment he would have been unable to take had he been a successful Liberal candidate.

The Trinity post was not to begin until October 1910. Russell was therefore still at Bagley Wood during the General Election of January, fought on the issue of the power of the Lords and with the Liberal cry of 'the peers versus the people'. 'I decided that I ought to help the Liberals as much as I could', he records, 'but I did not want to help the Member for the constituency in which I was living, as he had broken some pledges which I considered important. I therefore decided to help the Member for the neighbouring constituency across the river.' This was Philip Morrell.

During the campaign – in which Morrell lost his seat – Russell saw a good deal of the candidate and his wife, but it was more than a year later that he took a step that changed his life. In March 1911, he was to lecture at the Sorbonne. *En route* to the Continent he spent the night at the Morrell's home in Bedford Square; and here, after the other guests had left, the truth suddenly erupted. 'I was utterly unprepared for the flood of passion which he now poured out on me', Ottoline later wrote. 'My imagination was swept away, but not my heart, although it was very much moved and upset. All Bertie's eloquence was brought to bear on me, urging me as a matter of duty to give up everything for him, and go forth with him into a new life.' On this point Russell's account was much the same. 'I had lived a celibate life for nine years during which all my energies had been absorbed by *Principia Mathematica*', he wrote. 'Suddenly the long restraint gave way like the bursting of a dam. I found myself over-whelmingly and passionately in love.'

Russell's *affaire* with Lady Ottoline was to affect not only his personal and private life but also his public career and his ability to express himself on esoteric matters in terms that ordinary people could understand. He would have been able to do this anyway, but Ottoline's prompting – almost her tuition – raised it to the level of genius. But there were other important results. As the relationship deepened, Russell was brought into touch with the artistic and literary groups which Ottoline cultivated, and with the dissenting

Lytton Strachey, Russell, and Lady Ottoline's husband, Philip Morrell, at the Morrells' house, Garsington Manor, during the First World War.

Russell at Garsington Manor about 1916 with (left to right, standing) Augustine Birrell, unknown, Augustine Birrell's son, Aldous Huxley, Lytton Strachey, John Tresidder Sheppard; (sitting) Dorothy Brett, Russell, Julian Morrell [Lady Ottoline's daughter] and her dog Socrates.

Garsington Manor, the Elizabethan house outside Oxford which Philip Morrell bought in March 1913. The house was then in a state of decay, with chickens running through the rooms and the garden a wilderness. Time and money were needed for restoration, and not until May 1915 were the Morrells able to move in.

political circle which in 1914 maintained that it was in Britain's interest to stand aside from the war. The liaison led, moreover, to his writing some 2,000 letters between 1911 and 1938, frequently at the rate of three a day. Many, written in Russell's small and meticulous hand, were love-letters; but many more were letters in which he embodied his views on almost everything under the sun, outlined his daily life at Cambridge and gave vivid accounts of his meetings with some of the brilliant men of his day – Conrad, D. H. Lawrence, T. S. Eliot and, perhaps the most important to Russell himself, Ludwig Wittgenstein. Thus the correspondence described his development as it was happening, without the revisions of hindsight.

Attracted as she was by Russell, it was not until some weeks later that Ottoline became his mistress, and despite Russell's constant appeals she never showed the slightest sign of breaking up her marriage or of abdicating from the social position she occupied and enjoyed. The situation that developed in the summer of 1911 had a touch of farce. Russell told Alys and departed from the matrimonial home for Cambridge where his Trinity rooms were to be his base for the next five years. Ottoline told Philip, who acquiesced. But conventions had to be regarded and until Russell acquired a small flat near both the British Museum and the Morrells' home in Bedford Square, meetings had to be circumspect. Putney Heath, Richmond Park, Wimbledon Common and Hampstead Heath were among the favourite rendez-vous. The summer was fine and Russell noted: 'Providence has been very kind to us and evidently approves.'

Only a few close friends knew of the liaison, although the number increased with the Morrells' acquisition of Garsington Manor, on the outskirts of Oxford, and the growth of Ottoline's circle of artists and writers. Meanwhile Russell the academic continued his life as Trinity Lecturer, presiding over a section of the International Congress of Mathematicians, contributing to the *Monist* and *The Proceedings of the*

Lady Ottoline Morrell. 'Bertrand Russell is most fascinating', she wrote after meeting him in 1909. 'I don't think I have ever met anyone more attractive, but very alarming, so quick and clear-sighted, and supremely intellectual – cutting false and real asunder. Somebody called him "The Day of Judgment".'

Aristotelian Society, behaving in every way as would be expected of the man who was co-author of *Principia Mathematica*.

At the same time he was changing; the influence of Ottoline was creating or awakening in him an aesthetic appreciation that had previously been either non-existent or dormant. 'In my heart', he had once admitted to Berenson, 'the whole business about Art is external to me – I believe it with my intellect, but in feeling I am a good British Philistine.' Now he could write of his enjoyment at listening to Bach's Passion Music in Ely Cathedral, of the pleasure given by fine landscape; and in Italy, marvelling at the statue of Victory in Brescia, he could tell Ottoline how he always had 'a sense of being left outside the gates of Paradise when I see such things'. For a while he was tempted by her religious leanings away from the agnostic pessimism of 'A Free Man's Worship', and drafted 'Prisons', now lost, which appears from their correspondence to have included a variety of topics, including the way in which a new religion might enable men to escape from the prison of human life.

Under Ottoline's influence he also embarked on a novella, *The Perplexities of John Forstice*. This evolved after she had read a draft autobiography in which he had elaborated on the torments of his upbringing, the agonies of his marriage to Alys and the various steps in his intellectual development. Ottoline proposed that he should turn it into conversations between a young man and an old man. Forty years later Russell maintained that the novella had been modelled on Mallock's *The New Republic*. His book, to which Ottoline herself contributed some parts, was worked over a number of times, submitted for criticism to the Whiteheads and several other friends, and finally put away to be published only after Russell's death.

More important was the 'Shilling Shocker', as he called it, *The Problems of Philosophy*, written for the Home University Library. Much of it was read aloud to Ottoline when Russell was visiting the Morrells' country cottage in the Chilterns, and the clarity which still makes it one of the best short introductions to philosophy was no doubt the result of Ottoline's questions on points which she wanted explained.

The 'Shilling Shocker' began by asking, 'Is there any knowledge which is so certain that no reasonable man can doubt it?' The answer, Russell went on to demonstrate, was more complicated than it seemed, but he argued for a solution to the problem which assumed the existence of objects which are independent of our perception of them. In philosophy this is known as realism, and Russell thus revealed that the break with his Idealistic teachers was complete.

Even after the success of the 'Shilling Shocker', Russell was still virtually unknown outside the comparatively small circle of philosophers and mathematicians. Inside it he by now occupied an important position; his work was studied throughout the world and his fame drew to Cambridge the student who was to affect him more than any other man during these central years of his life. This was Ludwig

Ludwig Wittgenstein, the Austrian philosopher, in G. E. Moore's Cambridge garden. 'He has the theoretical passion *very* strongly – it is a very rare passion & one is glad to find it,' wrote Russell after Wittgenstein had become his pupil in 1911. 'He doesn't want to prove this or that, but to find out how things really are.'

Wittgenstein, an Austrian who had graduated in engineering in Berlin-Charlottenberg, worked as a research student in aeronautics in Manchester University and there, intrigued by the problems involved in designing a jet reaction propeller, had turned to the philosophical foundations of mathematics. In October 1911 Wittgenstein arrived at Trinity to study under Russell.

From the first, Russell was fascinated by Wittgenstein, 'perhaps the most perfect example [I have] ever known of genius as traditionally conceived, passionate, profound, intense and dominating'. The student not only listened intently to the master but, when lectures were finished, pestered him with questions. 'My German [sic] friend threatens to be an affliction', Russell once complained to Ottoline, adding subsequently such comments on his student as 'very argumentative and tiresome' and 'armour-plated against all assaults of reasoning'.

As Russell became aware of the intellect that lay concealed beneath the implacable self-confidence, his attitude changed. 'I am getting to like him', Ottoline was told; 'he is literary, very musical, pleasant-mannered (being an Austrian) and I *think* really intelligent.' All doubts about the intelligence were swept away after Wittgenstein had confessed that he was havering between philosophy and aviation, asked Russell's advice, and produced a short paper to show his mettle. 'Very good, much better than my English pupils do', Russell had decided. 'I shall certainly encourage him. Perhaps he will do great things.'

The month was January 1912 and from now onwards until the late summer of 1913, when Wittgenstein left Cambridge to settle in Norway, he and Russell met, worked and discussed philosophy increasingly as equals. Wittgenstein was, Russell remarked in the spring of 1912, the only man he had ever met with 'a real taste for philosophical scepticism' and as early as May he was proud of his student's acclaim, writing to Ottoline, '*He* thinks my paper on matter the best thing I have done – but he has only read the beginning & the end.'

The admiration grew. Wittgenstein, Russell was certain, would live to carry on Russell's ideas. He was a man for the future, the first into whom Russell was to put his hopes, only to watch the hopes evaporate. Disappointment came in the summer of 1913 when Russell was at work on a major discussion of Theory of Knowledge. He began it early in May, aimed to write 10 pages a day, and within a month had written 350. At first, all went splendidly. He was 'as happy as a king', 'living the life of one possessed', and was confident that the work was 'amazingly sincere – there is absolutely nothing "clever" anywhere, except possibly a few words on the very first page, which I shall alter some day', he told Ottoline.

During the last days of May all was changed. Wittgenstein called on Russell. Russell showed him a crucial part of his manuscript, and the student told the master that it was 'all wrong', that he had tried it 'and knew it wouldn't work'.

It would be too much to claim that Russell was demolished. But within a month he was writing: 'All that has gone wrong with me comes from Wittgenstein's attack on my work – I have only just realized this. It was very difficult to be honest about it, as it makes a large part of the book I meant to write impossible for years to come probably . . . the first time in my life that I have failed in honesty over work.' And three years later he was describing Wittgenstein's criticism as 'an event of first-rate importance in my life [which] affected everything I have done since. I saw he was right, and I saw that I could not hope ever again to do fundamental work in philosophy. My impulse was shattered, like a wave dashed to pieces against a break-water. I became filled with utter despair.'

Russell abandoned the book, although six later articles in the *Monist* were almost certainly parts of it. The essence of Wittgenstein's criticism is not entirely certain. It appears, however, to have been that Russell's sophisticated theory of judgment had omitted what Wittgenstein believed to be an essential factor. 'He saw', it has been stated, 'that Russell had omitted the binding factor, the element which would combine the disparate constituents into a significant whole, and make it impossible for a piece of nonsense – such as "the table penholders the book" – to result from the formula.'

Judging by Wittgenstein's subsequent *Tractatus Logico-Philosophicus*, the objections may have been more broadly based, but they were, in any case, sufficient to drive Russell into one of his more than usually deep troughs of depression. He began to recover during a long holiday tour of northern Italy, was driven down again by a belief that he and Ottoline should part, and returned to Cambridge in September almost as distraught as before.

However, he had an important task to which he could devote himself. It was not only in Britain that his reputation as a philosopher had grown with the publication of *Principia Mathematica*. In the United States, *The Principles of Mathematics* was widely read by supporters of the New Realism, the American opposition to Idealism, and Russell was now invited to give the Lowell Lectures in Cambridge, Massachusetts, and to give a course at Harvard. He hesitated a long while before accepting, unhappy at being separated from Ottoline for what would be three months. Eventually he agreed to a date in March 1914 and in the autumn of 1913 began work on the lectures. He intended that the subject should be the place of Good and Evil in the Universe but was asked to make it less religious. Unabashed, he noted to Ottoline that he could 'give them the same stuff as "the scope & limits of scientific method" – perhaps the need of some restraint will improve it'. Having completed the task in twenty-five days, he revised and added to the work, then changed the order of the lectures and re-grouped them around the problems of the external world.

After a break in Rome for Christmas, he returned to Trinity and embarked on a concentrated programme of writing which was enormous, even for Russell. One reason was that he wished to keep from his mind the awful fact that he would soon be parting from Ottoline for three months. The burst of work produced a 12,000-word paper on 'The Relation of Sense-Data to Physics' that he was to read before the New York Philosophical Society; 'Mysticism & Logic'; a preface to Poincaré's *Science and Method*; and the lectures he was to read at Harvard.

He crossed the Atlantic during the second week of March, his voyage made agreeable by the company of Sir Francis Younghusband, the explorer, since each man found that he admired the very different qualities of the other. At Harvard his hosts regarded the mathematician and philosopher with respect and the heir to an earldom with awe. From the first he was lionized, and between lecturing at the Lowell Institute and giving six lectures a week at Harvard, was expected to find time for much socializing. He was

Harvard, where Russell lectured in 1914. Here Russell was lionized, one reason being that the New Realism – the American opposition to Idealism which had developed in the first years of the century – was now a popular movement in American philosophy.

Right: The young T. S. Eliot, whom Russell first met at Harvard in 1914. 'Proficient in Plato, intimate with French literature from Villon to Vildrach' was Russell's verdict – 'very capable of a certain exquisiteness of appreciation, but lacking in the crude insistent passion that one must have in order to achieve anything. However, he is the only pupil of that sort I have; all the others are vigorous intelligent barbarians.'

taken to supper with Roscoe Pound, the scholar soon to become head of Harvard's Faculty of Law. He listened to Alfred Noyes's poems read by Noyes himself and considered them banal. He met John Dewey, already famous for his work in philosophy and educational theory, and was approached for advice by one of his Harvard pupils, a then unknown T. S. Eliot.

Russell admitted that he liked the adulation – although 'it gives me less pleasure than I thought it would' – but was critical of most Americans. At Harvard *none* of those he met had any quality, while as for Bostonians, Russell's description was 'rich, over-eating, selfish feeble pigs'. This bludgeoning criticism of those who at least were doing their best was perhaps a by-product of the fact that they were keeping him from Ottoline. But a deeper irritation is suggested by his description of one dinner-party at which he met 'the kind of people who are frightfully proud of their ancient lineage because they go back to 1776' – no very distant date for one whose maternal grandmother had been hobnobbing with the Young Pretender's widow.

In April there came a break in New York and then a return to Harvard where, to Russell's huge relief, he found three letters from Ottoline awaiting him. 'Thank Heaven half of [the visit] is over', he wrote without delay. Shortly afterwards he left for Bryn Mawr, to which he had been invited despite the opposition of Dr Carey Thomas; for Johns Hopkins; Princeton; and Smith College, Northampton. In Northampton he read 'Mysticism & Logic', an essay that arose from his discussions on religion with Ottoline and in which he admitted that 'the greatest men who have been philosophers have felt the need both of science and of mysticism'. The tour increased Russell's standing in American academic circles and was thus to be of significance during the next few years when he sought support in the United States for his attitude to the war.

After Smith College there were a few more weeks at Harvard and then the return to England; a return, however, by way of Ann Arbor, where he gave a single lecture, and then Chicago, where he stayed with an eminent gynaecologist, Dr Dudley. Helen Dudley, one of the doctor's four daughters, had studied under Gilbert Murray at Oxford a few years earlier. She had met Russell a few times and on learning that he was to visit Ann Arbor had invited him to stay at her parents' home – 200 miles away but hardly distant by American standards. 'She met me at the station', he later wrote, 'and I at once felt more at home with her than I had with anybody else that I had met in America. I found that she wrote rather good poetry, and that her feeling for literature was remarkable and unusual. I spent two nights under her parents' roof, and the second I spent with her. Her three sisters mounted guard to give warning if either of the parents approached.'

He broke the news to Ottoline as casually as he could, saying that he did not want her 'to think that this will make the very *smallest* difference in my feeling towards you, beyond removing the irritation of unsatisfied instinct'. But he added that Helen Dudley would be coming to England as soon as she could.

Russell returned to Britain in the summer of 1914 with one personal problem: how was he to explain away Helen Dudley to Ottoline who, however obliging, might wonder where his real affections lay? Of Helen, Russell was to claim in his autobiography that 'the shock of the war killed my passion for her . . . If the war had not intervened, the plan which we formed in Chicago might have brought great happiness to us both. I feel still the sorrow of this tragedy.'

His letters to Ottoline reveal a very different story. As early as 23 June, six weeks before the outbreak of war and five days before Sarajevo, he was attempting to explain: 'I am less fond of H.D. than I have tried to persuade myself that I was; her affection for me has made me do my utmost to respond.' Before mid-July, with the war as yet only a cloud on the horizon, the explanation becomes more explicit: 'if she came to care for someone else that seemed capable of helping her, I should be glad.' His problem was increased when he learned that Miss Dudley was in fact to follow him across the Atlantic as they had arranged in Chicago and was to arrive in Britain on 8

One of Russell's comments to Lady Ottoline Morrell about Helen Dudley, the young American girl who was to follow him across the Atlantic after he returned to Britain from the United States in the summer of 1914. Her sister Katherine was later responsible for smuggling Russell's appeal to President Wilson out of Britain when his mail was being intercepted by the authorities.

August 'unless', he added with expectation to Ottoline, 'captured by Germans'.

Helen Dudley safely arrived in England with her father, who returned to America after a few weeks. She knew nothing of Russell's real relationship with Ottoline and stayed with the Morrells for a while in Bedford Square. Russell disentangled himself with some difficulty but ultimate success.

The ease with which he was eventually able to shuffle off the young girl – 'Never mind if she is hurt', he remarked to Ottoline after she had found work in London for Helen – was an example of what has been called his 'peculiar self-absorbed ruthlessness of a young child, capable of great affection, and of passion, but not of any serious interest in other people'. It was also an illustration of the ease with which his sexual appetite could lead him into escapades which slipped from his personal control.

None of this should disguise his preoccupation with the war which began on 4 August, although his first reactions were more ambivalent than is generally realized. To Lucy Donnelly, an old friend at Bryn Mawr, he wrote that now that it had begun 'there is nothing for it but to prosecute it'. And he took it for granted, he wrote to Ottoline, that

Lucy Donnelly of Bryn Mawr College, a contemporary and friend of Russell's first wife Alys, with whom he maintained a half-century's close but platonic friendship.

Philip would 'not oppose Government while the war lasts, and that he recognizes the need of prosecuting it with all vigour now we are in'.

A further indication that Russell's views were, despite the attacks on him, by no means pro-German, is given in a letter written to an American in November 1914 and justifying an earlier letter to the *Nation*.

> I wrote as an advocate of peace, not as an advocate of the German Government, which I consider far [Russell first wrote 'infinitely'] more to blame than the Government of England; I wrote as an advocate of humanity, not as a defender of the violation of Belgian neutrality and the devastation of Belgian towns and villages, which I consider an unspeakable crime; I wrote as an advocate of justice and truth, not as a friend to the German hysteria beside which our English hysteria seems almost an approach to sanity . . . Now that war exists, I consider the victory of the Allies of great importance to mankind: the defeat of democracy and the triumph of the Bismarckian tradition would, I believe, postpone for a long time the political progress of civilization.

Despite these sentiments Russell maintained, and was to maintain for the rest of his life, that Britain could and should have remained neutral, a sentiment held in the country in August 1914 far more generally than is appreciated today. It was a sentiment that alienated him from many of his former friends; from Gilbert Murray, condemned as 'squashy as a slug' for his support of Grey, the Foreign Minister; and from Alfred and Evelyn Whitehead. 'I feel as if my relations with the whole family could never again be quite the same', he told Ottoline.

Before the end of 1914 Russell had joined the Union of Democratic Control, an organization that was to survive both the First and the Second World Wars, contemplated a lecture tour of the United States during which he planned to counter official British propaganda, and had opened negotiations for what was to be a series of articles for the influential *Atlantic Monthly*. 'War: The Offspring of Fear', written for the UDC, was burned in Cambridge, one of those present saying that it should have been burned by the public hangman.

By the first months of 1915 Russell had decided to devote himself entirely to anti-war propaganda. The result was that when his lectureship ended and Trinity decided to elect him to a research fellowship, he felt unable to accept; instead, his lectureship was renewed. Before the year was out he cut his links with the Liberals, swung away from the UDC and began to work for the larger and far more activist No-Conscription Fellowship. At this point he came under the scrutiny of the Government, and with good reason. The anti-war movement of the First World War was supported by many men, and women, of sincere faith and much courage. What it tended to lack was those such as Russell who had the intellect and the will to tweak authority's tail, who could judge to a nicety when the powers-that-be could be induced to make fools of themselves. The Government knew this and from an early stage regarded Russell as an enemy

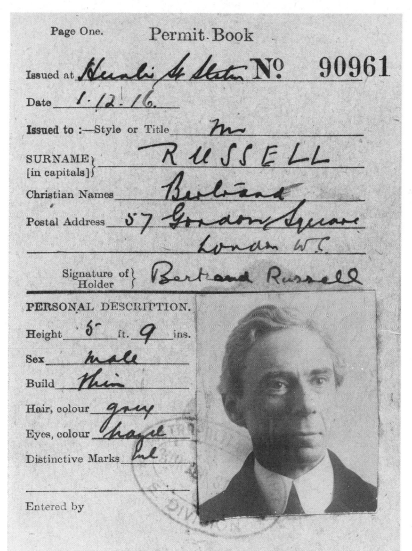

A page of the Permit Book issued to Russell after he had been banned from travelling to certain areas of Britain during the First World War.

to be handled with care. On one occasion the Permanent Under-Secretary at the Home Office, advising against prosecuting Russell, admitted: 'He writes and speaks with a good deal of misguided cleverness. . . . He would make a clever defence and would publish it as a pamphlet.'

If Russell's ability to make intellectual rings round officialdom frequently gave a boost to the men and women in the No-Conscription movement, there was another way in which he helped the pacifist cause: by his family and social contacts with what would today be called the Establishment. Few members of the movement had lines open to those who made decisions. Russell, on the contrary, moved in circles where the Prime Minister could drop in without causing surprise; his brother was a member of the House of Lords, and although a rather racketty member could at least catch the ear of others. These things help, even in the Britain of the 1980s; they helped considerably more during the First World War.

Through Ottoline, at whose Garsington Manor he was to meet the Prime Minister and his friends – 'a queer mix-up', as Maynard Keynes was to call it – Russell also met D. H. Lawrence, a confrontation of personalities which was to have at least one important outcome. This was the publication of Russell's first attempt to set out a political philosophy. He had discussed with Lawrence the prospects of hiring a hall in London where each of them could lecture on politics, ethics, and religion, and sent Lawrence a draft of what he thought his own lectures should contain. It was returned without delay – with the occasional 'No' marked across whole paragraphs and one 'Must' underlined no less than fifteen times. For some months Russell put aside the idea. Then, in the early autumn of 1915, he turned to it once again. 'I wrote [the lectures] as a human being who suffered from the state of the world', he later stated. 'I wished to find some way of improving it, and was anxious to speak in plain terms to others who had similar feelings.' His thesis was that the impulses which he believed moulded men's lives more effectively than conscious purpose were either possessive or creative, with the State, war and property being examples of the first and education, marriage and religion exemplifying the second. Liberation of creativeness should be the aim, and he went on to suggest how this might be achieved when the war was over.

D. H. Lawrence about 1912. He and Russell, who had been introduced to each other by Lady Ottoline, had planned to collaborate in a series of political lectures – eventually written by Russell as *Principles of Social Reconstruction* – but had strongly disagreed about what they should contain.

Caxton Hall, Westminster, where early in 1916 Russell gave the lectures later published as *Principles of Social Reconstruction*. 'It is splendid the way he sticks at nothing', Lytton Strachey said of the lectures, ' – Governments, religions, laws, property, even Good Form itself – down they go like ninepins – it is a charming sight.'

The lectures were given on eight evenings in Caxton Hall, Westminster, and to steadily more numerous audiences. Published as *Principles of Social Reconstruction*, they made considerable impact in the United States where they appeared as *Why Men Fight: A Method of Abolishing the International Duel*, and led to the proposal that Russell should lecture on the same subject at Harvard. He was to be stopped by the British Government from giving the lectures, an admission that he had now reached an almost unique position in the official demonology.

From the end of 1915 Russell gave dedicated, and in the view of Whitehall, worrying support to the No-Conscription Fellowship. He spoke on their platforms, he edited their journal, *The Tribunal*, and he frequently wrote hectoring editorials for it. He made for the Fellowship a propaganda tour of South Wales. To the often woolly good intentions of palpably honest men he added a stiffening ramrod of logic which the authorities soon not only detested but feared. As the fighting went on and the casualty lists showed that a confined European war had turned into a national blood-letting, Russell became one of the most hated men in Britain.

There were two highlights, the first in 1916, the second in 1918. In the spring of 1916 Russell wrote a leaflet dealing with the imprisonment of a young conscientious objector, Ernest Everett. After six men had been sent to prison for distributing it, he wrote a letter published by *The Times* which ended, 'if anyone is to be prosecuted, I am the person primarily responsible'. The Government obligingly prosecuted, 'the very thing I wanted', as Russell wrote to Ottoline. It was no vain boast; one of his regrets was that he was too old to be called up, with all the possibilities of embarrassing the authorities that this would offer. 'It is maddening', he protested, 'not to be liable.'

Although the court which heard the Everett case imposed a fine of £100 or 61 days in prison, Russell's hoped-for martyrdom was missed. He declined to pay, but friends unexpectedly bought his £100-worth of books when a Distress for non-payment was issued. Thus prison was avoided and his books immediately returned by the friends. Then, although both the Government and Russell had failed in their aim of getting him locked up – 'I am not anxious to secure an acquittal', he had told Ottoline – Trinity provided adequate publicity by sacking Russell from his lectureship.

Many Fellows of Trinity objected, some from the battle-front. Hilton Young, later Lord Kennet, wrote from HMS Centaur, pleading that England should remain 'a place in which the Russells whom fate grants us from time to time should be free to stimulate and annoy us unpersecuted'. Others pointed out that although the German government had done its best to have the pacifist Professor Förster sacked from the University of Munich, the university had refused. The Government had failed to give the Germans a propaganda victory by imprisoning Russell; Trinity succeeded by other means.

The case was to have another repercussion. Russell had been offered a lectureship by Harvard on terms which would enable him to give not only a course on philosophy but another course based on the *Principles of Social Reconstruction*. He was loath to be separated from Ottoline once more; but, as he told her, he could make a clear £400 profit from the visit and this would make it possible for him 'to have a nice cottage in the Chilterns, near Prince's Risborough, & pay for you to come all the way in a motor car if you would visit me there'.

Russell accepted. But even before 'the Everett case' had begun the British Ambassador in Washington, Sir Cecil Spring Rice, was suggesting to the Foreign Office that Russell 'might be warned that Germans will circulate any anti-British utterances he may make there'. The authorities, who needed some good reason for refusing Russell a passport, had their difficulties removed by the successful prosecution. 'Mr. Russell', the Foreign Office was thereby enabled to cable Washington, 'has been convicted under the Defence of the Realm Act for writing an undesirable pamphlet and no passport will be issued to him to proceed to the United States.'

It is quite clear from official documents available that Russell's war with the authorities gave them cause for considerable concern. He had the advantage over many modern dissidents in that he operated in a country where official violence was ruled out and where he found it easy to confuse a heavy-footed bureaucracy. One example was his open letter to Woodrow Wilson, who had been re-elected on the slogan 'He kept us out of war'. Russell had no difficulty in writing an eloquent 1,200-word appeal to the President which urged him to make every effort towards a negotiated peace. Getting it to America was another matter, since Russell correctly suspected that his mail was being opened and read. However, Helen Dudley's sister Katherine, now living in London, was about to return to America. It was extremely unlikely that any American, let alone an American woman, would be searched on leaving Britain and Katherine Dudley arrived in New York on 20 December with the letter concealed in her clothes.

Three days later *The New York Times* printed Russell's appeal in full under the front-page banner headline: 'Mysterious Girl Brings Russell's Peace Plea Here; Famous English Philosopher and Mathematician Asks Wilson to Stop War Ere Europe Perishes.' The letter itself was put before Wilson by Walter Lippmann, his unofficial press attaché and lately a philosophy student at Harvard. It was, according to a worried cable from Spring Rice to the Foreign Office, 'supposed to have received the President's earnest consideration'.

Russell's support for the No-Conscription Fellowship was to have one outcome totally different from his trial and his dismissal from Trinity. On 31 July 1916, he arrived at Lavender Hill police station in South London where Clifford Allen (later Lord Allen of Hurtwood), a founder of the N-CF, was to be charged under the Military Service

Clifford Allen, later Lord Allen of Hurtwood, chairman of the No-Conscription Fellowship, was sent to prison more than once during the First World War. 'Very able as an organiser and leader' wrote Russell after hearing Allen speak; ' – not attractive personally, but capable of becoming a power, and sure to be always on the right side.'

Lady Constance Malleson, often known by her stage-name of Colette O'Niel. She became Russell's mistress in 1916; although the relationship continued for only a few years, they remained close friends for the rest of Russell's life.

Opposite: Bertrand Russell at Garsington Manor in 1918.

Act. In the waiting room there was a slight auburn-haired girl of 21, also a friend of Allen. Her path and Russell's were to cross and inter-cross for the next 50 years; more than once his feelings for her nearly changed the course of his life.

Lady Constance Malleson, waiting like Russell to give Allen moral support, was the younger daughter of the 5th Earl Annesley. She had begun a career as an actress under the name Colette O'Niel, and in 1915 had married Miles Malleson, a former fellow student at the Royal Academy of Dramatic Art. Malleson had enlisted in 1914, been invalided home, and had then decided to oppose the war. By 1916 both he and Colette, as she was generally known, were working for the N-CF.

On 31 July, there was only a brief encounter between Russell and Colette. It was six weeks before they met again, at a dinner where a

small group of Left-wingers discussed the war. Then, ten days later, both attended the annual N-CF Convention. After it, Russell and Colette dined together and then walked back to her flat where they became lovers. 'At first', Russell later wrote, 'I had great difficulty in shutting Ottoline out of my feeling, but within a few months Colette absorbed me completely and for a time I was completely happy with her.'

The happiness did not last, mainly due to Colette's promiscuity. Relations were broken, renewed, then broken again. In his auto-biography Russell gives the impression that the *affaire* ended when, after five years, he finally abandoned her and she 'woke up one fine morning in 1921 to find life finished'. The truth was very different and at least until 1948 Russell's life was to be intermittently chequered by restoration of links with Colette. They should, he once wrote, 'never have parted'.

By 1917 Russell's reputation as a pacifist agitator had in the minds of the general public quite outstripped his renown as a conjuror with abstruse mathematical symbols that only a few could understand. And even in Cambridge there persisted an uncomfortable feeling that a man of such impeccable intellectual activity really should not take up a provocative stance when, surely, the war now had to be fought to a finish. Russell remained unmoved, still feeling, as he had felt earlier, that he 'had heard the voice of God. I knew that it was my business to protest, however futile protest might be.'

Then, in the autumn of 1917, he resigned from the No-Conscription Fellowship. He still opposed the war and he still opposed con-scription. Since he was still as valuable as ever to the movement, the action looks at first like retreat. It was in fact the result of the logical reasoning which Russell always believed, in the face of the evidence, could and should be utilized by the rest of mankind. He had welcomed the Kerensky Revolution despite the bloodshed involved, attended the Royal Albert Hall meeting held to celebrate it, and travelled to Leeds to speak at a rally called to plan ways of co-ordinating British work with the Russians. To Russell this was incompatible with membership of an organization which based itself on the sacredness of human life, and he therefore wrote to the N-CF Committee saying: 'If the "sacredness of human life" means that force must *never* be used to upset bad systems of Government, to put an end to wars and despotism, and to bring liberty to the oppressed, then I cannot honestly subscribe to it.'

There were, it is true, other reasons for Russell's resignation which it would be unfair to conceal. He thought himself unadaptable to administrative work. He thought the calibre of members of the N-CF executive too low. He wanted to get back to philosophy, and if there was any intellectual time to spare he believed that he should devote it to the political problems of the peace. These all counted. But, most important of all, he was not a man to sail under false colours. Devoting all his energies to a body which believed in the sacredness of

human life while at the same time supporting the Russian Revolution was too much.

Once comparatively clear of work for the N-CF, Russell turned to a series of eight lectures which he was to give in London early in 1918 and which were to be published as *The Philosophy of Logical Atomism*. They were, as he was to write in a characteristic prefatory note, 'very largely concerned with explaining certain ideas which I learnt from my friend and former pupil Ludwig Wittgenstein'. In essence, logical atomism had been forced upon him 'in the course of thinking about the philosophy of mathematics'. The process that he had there carried out with symbols could now, he maintained, be used with equally good effect when considering non-mathematical philosophy; the result would show that its problems were the result of slovenly use of language and were amenable to solution if the more formal methods of logical atomism were followed.

Russell finished outlining his lectures on *The Philosophy of Logical Atomism* while spending the Christmas of 1917 at Garsington. And here, in the company of Ottoline's sophisticated friends, he threw off

Crowds breaking into a meeting held on 28 July 1917 in the Brotherhood Church, Southgate Road, Islington, to welcome the Russian Revolution. 'The mob got in by smashing the doors, before our meeting had begun,' Russell told Lady Ottoline. '. . . I realized vividly how ghastly the spirit of violence is, & how utterly I repudiate it, on whatever side it may be. The mob is a terrible thing when it wants blood.'

Russell at Garsington Manor. It was here, at Christmas 1917, that he mischievously suggested that US troops might be used to intimidate strikers in Britain. Repeated in *The Tribunal*, the assertion led to a six-month prison sentence.

Opposite: Russell in 1918 outside Bow Street Court, where he had been sentenced for 'having in a printed publication made certain statements likely to prejudice His Majesty's relations with the United States of America'.

one of his typically mischievous suggestions: if the American forces being concentrated in southern England were not efficient against the Germans, they could surely intimidate strikers in Britain.

The remark, harmless enough in a company where no one took it seriously, was to have unexpected repercussions. When Russell resigned from the N-CF he made it clear that he would always be willing to help out in an emergency. One arrived shortly after Christmas. He had given up his regular weekly article for *The Tribunal*, but no substitute was available for the first few issues of 1918 and he agreed to fill the unexpected gap. Here, commenting on the American troops, he remembered the Christmas discussion at Garsington and hastily wrote that 'whether or not they will prove efficient against the Germans, [they] will no doubt be capable of intimidating strikers, an occupation to which the American Army is accustomed when at home'.

Shortly afterwards Russell was charged at Bow Street with having made statements 'likely to prejudice His Majesty's relations with the United States of America'. Significantly, the US Ambassador in London, Walter Page, appears to have supported his military attaché's refusal to give evidence for the British Government. However, the pacifist who had stumped the country to some effect for more

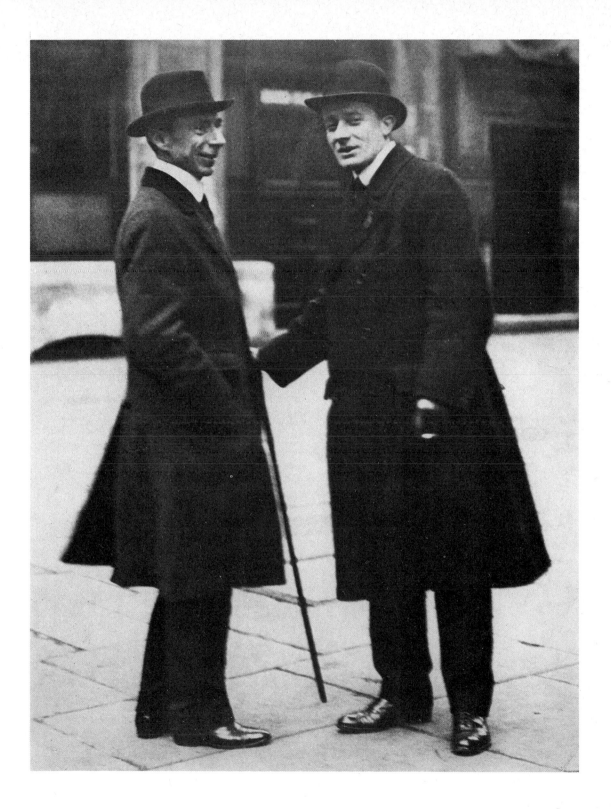

than three years was now given a six-month prison sentence for a few incautious words.

Russell decided to finish one job before he began his sentence: this was *Roads to Freedom: Socialism, Anarchism and Syndicalism*. The book had been commissioned by an American publisher and Russell told Leonard Woolf that he had undertaken it 'solely for the sake of filthy lucre'. This seems to have been one of Russell's misleadingly throwaway statements, since the text shows every sign of having been written with enthusiastic conviction that Guild Socialism offered the best chance of progress in the peace that lay not so very far ahead.

The book was published shortly after the Armistice in November 1918, ran through three editions within fourteen months and was then reprinted twice within the next three years. It successfully assuaged the post-war demand for information on ways of curing what one reviewer called 'the unhappiness of the world' and it was remarkable, in view of its subject, that it was praised not only by *The Times*, but by *The Christian World* and *Christian Commonwealth*.

Whether Russell would have been allowed to finish *Roads to Freedom* in prison is not known. However, his hardship there was to be limited. By convincing the authorities that he had important philosophical work to do, he was allowed to serve his sentence in the First Division. As a result he had books and writing materials as required, three visitors a week, his own food sent in from outside the prison, and, for 6d. a week, the services of another prisoner to relieve him 'from the performance of unaccustomed tasks or offices'.

Prisoner 2917, as he had become, made the best of Brixton Prison. 'I had no engagements, no difficult decisions to make, no fear of callers, no interruptions to my work', he later wrote. Before long he was informing his brother that he had nearly finished the 70,000 words of an *Introduction to Mathematical Philosophy*, a book giving in comparatively simple terms for the layman the results of *The Principles of Mathematics* and *Principia Mathematica*.

Once this was out of the way he found his thoughts, as he was later to write, 'turning to theory of knowledge and to those parts of psychology and of linguistics which seemed relevant to that subject. This was a more or less permanent change in my philosophical interests.' The first result was *The Analysis of Mind* (1921), Russell's attempt to describe mind in terms which were in accord with the modern discoveries of psychology.

In prison Russell had time and tranquillity to carry on his professional work. His only worry concerned Colette, and his release from Brixton in the second half of September 1918 was followed by clashes in which he accused her of infidelity, by reconciliations, and then by further clashes. He spent some days at Garsington, some in London with his brother, not knowing what to do or where next to turn. On 11 November, as the maroons boomed out the peace, he was in London. 'The crowd rejoiced and I also rejoiced', he wrote. 'But I remained as solitary as before.'

Brixton Prison, where Russell began to serve a six-month sentence early in May 1918. He arrived in a taxi, regretting that the authorities had not arranged for a Black Maria. The sentence was to be served in the First Division and Russell planned to spend four hours each day on philosophical writing, four hours on philosophical reading and four hours on general reading.

Armistice Day, 11 November 1918. Russell, who was in London, commented: 'The crowd rejoiced and I also rejoiced. But I remained as solitary as before.'

What had he achieved? He himself believed it was very little. 'I saw that all I had done had been totally useless except to myself', he wrote. 'I had not saved a single life or shortened the war by one minute. I had not succeeded in doing anything to diminish the bitterness which caused the Treaty of Versailles.' Yet if all this were true, he had nevertheless given a measure of confidence to many conscientious objectors fearful of what was to befall them, determined to do what they believed was right, and encouraged by the knowledge that a man of Russell's standing was prepared to support them. In addition, he had by his stand, and even more by his writing, made it possible for the objectors in the Second World War to be treated less savagely than those of the First.

The Armistice left Russell solitary and stranded. He had done his duty by deliberately seeking imprisonment but few people had been particularly impressed; in any case, 'the Cause' had ended with the maroons of November. *The Analysis of Mind*, begun in prison, was soon completed, and he filled in time with reviewing and with a job lot of

Dora Black, Russell's second wife, at Garsington Manor. They had first met during the latter part of the First World War, then again in Dorset where Miss Black stayed with Russell and a party of friends at Newlands Farm, Lulworth.

journalistic articles which had little to do with philosophy. For eighteen months, until visits to Russia and to China helped crystallize his intentions, he remained irresolute and undecided.

If his professional life appeared to be foundering, his private life was in a state of even greater chaos than usual. For Ottoline there remained the great affection which was to last all her life. For Colette there remained a passion forever distressed by her inability to remain faithful to him. 'Colette's capacity for being in love with several people at once was astonishing', he was later to write. 'I would get long letters from her reading like love-letters and ending up in the last sentence by remarking that she was passionately in love with someone else. In theory I did not object, but practice did not follow the theory. I loved Colette passionately, but after the first her promiscuity tortured me.' And for Dora Black, a young woman who swam into his ken during the first summer of the peace, there quickly grew up a considerable love.

In June 1919 Russell and a mathematical colleague from Cambridge, John Littlewood, began a three-month holiday near Lulworth

Above: John Maynard Keynes, who while the principal representative of the Treasury at the Paris Peace Conference in 1919, was approached both by Russell and by Wittgenstein, a prisoner-of-war in Italy. As a result, the two men met to discuss Wittgenstein's *Tractatus Logico-Philosophicus,* a copy of which Wittgenstein had already sent to Russell.

Above right: Dorothy Wrinch had joined a small group in Russell's rooms in 1916 to discuss symbolic logic, the prospects for the pacifist cause and the outcome of the war. In the summer of 1919 she visited Russell in Dorset with Dora Black.

Opposite: Lulworth Cove, Dorset. It was in the nearby Newlands Farm that Russell read Arthur Eddington's report on Einstein's General Theory of Relativity. He was so overwhelmed by Eddington's argument that he one day exclaimed in exasperation: 'to think I've spent my life on *muck*!'

on the Dorset coast. To the farm they had leased among 'the big simple eternal things – the sound of the sea on the shingle, the cry of gulls, moonlight on the waves, the setting sun on cliffs', as he described it to Ottoline, there came many visitors. Among them was Dorothy Wrinch, a wartime pupil of Russell's who was to become a distinguished mathematician, and her friend Miss Dora Black. Russell dutifully reported to Ottoline that Miss Black was 'nice' but thought it unlikely that he would 'take up' with her. However, there were second thoughts. 'By this time my desire to have children had become overwhelming', he later wrote, 'and I had almost begun to feel that Fate was going to interfere with the realization of my hopes. I found Dora entirely willing to have children and I became her lover.'

At Lulworth Russell did more than decide that a marriage to Dora Black offered a prospect of happiness. He also started the machinery that was to end in publication of Wittgenstein's *Tractatus Logico-Philosophicus,* the aphoristic book which attempted to show the way in which the language of *Principia Mathematica* could be used to solve certain philosophic problems. Having heard a few months earlier that his former pupil was a prisoner-of-war in Italy, he had invoked the help of Maynard Keynes, an old friend and by now the principal representative of the British Treasury at the Paris Peace Conference. The outcome was the arrival of Wittgenstein's manuscript. Russell and Dorothy Wrinch read it, then despatched a series of questions to the author. However, before their arrival at the prisoner-of-war camp, Wittgenstein had received a copy of Russell's

64

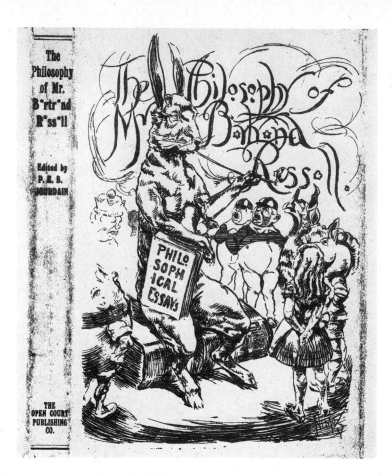

The jacket of Philip Jourdain's *The Philosophy of Mr B*rtr*nd R*ss*ll*, a *jeu d'esprit* published in 1918 that consisted of forty-three very short chapters each of which developed a philosophical joke. There were also twenty appendices, containing quotations from Lewis Carroll and linking such matters as Russell's treatment of non-existent entities and the White Knight.

Introduction to Mathematical Philosophy. The reaction was Wittgensteinian. 'I should never have believed that what I dictated to Moore in Norway six years ago would pass over you so completely without trace', Russell was brusquely told. 'In short, I am afraid it might be very difficult for me to reach an understanding with you.'

Nevertheless, Wittgenstein was still anxious to see Russell and the two men later met in the Hague. Russell did his best to find a publisher for the manuscript and went so far as to write an introduction to it. Having failed, he handed the task to Dorothy Wrinch, who after much effort persuaded Wilhelm Ostwald to publish it in his journal, *Annalen der Natur-philosophie.*

In December 1920 Russell's professional problems appeared to have been solved. A letter to the Council of Trinity, signed by twenty-eight Fellows, had asked for his reinstatement and the Council thereupon invited him to accept a five-year Lectureship in Logic and the Principles of Mathematics. He accepted, and was expected to begin a course of lectures the following October. Here, at last, there would once more be a hitching-post for his life. But personal events were again to do their worst.

Throughout the first months of 1920 Russell havered between the attractions of Colette, to whom he described various disputations with Dora, and of Dora with whom, he had already told Ottoline, he intended 'to begin a common life'. It was not quite clear whether this meant marriage and Russell knew that if it did not, then the conventions of the times would force him to relinquish his Trinity lectureship.

These problems were shovelled to one side when, in the spring, he was invited to join a Labour delegation to the Soviet Union. He seized with both hands the opportunity to see for himself what was happening in the wake of the revolution he had so ardently welcomed. He returned in June, 1920, totally disillusioned. He had been singled out as a guest by Kamenov, President of the Moscow Soviet, given numerous privileges denied to more plebeian members of the delegation, and granted an hour with Lenin who said the peasants were roaming about stringing up their former landlords to the nearest trees. Lenin guffawed at the thought. 'I didn't like that

The British Labour delegation to the Soviet Union in 1920 seen among Russian soldiers. Russell accompanied the delegation – although not a member of it – and met both Trotsky and Lenin. 'He preferred to go about himself,' Emma Goldman, the American anarchist and journalist then in Russia, commented of Russell. 'He also showed no elation over the honour of being quartered in a palace and fed on special morsels. Suspicious person, that Russell, the Bolsheviki whispered.'

May 19. Morning, visit to Marchand, former correspondent of Figaro, now Bolshevik, though not materialist, agreeable, not important. Afternoon, walk round Kremlin — extraordinary beautiful churches. Evening, interview with Lenin, one hour. His room is very bare — a big desk, some maps on the walls, 2 book-cases, one easy chair for visitors. Throughout the time I was there, a sculptor was working on a bust of him. Conversation in English, very fairly good. He is friendly & apparently simple — entirely without a trace of hauteur, a great contrast to Trotsky. Nothing in his manner or bearing suggests the man who has power. He looks at his visitor very close, & screws up one eye. He laughs a great deal; at first, his laugh seems merely friendly & jolly, but gradually one finds it grim. He is dictatorial, calm, incapable of fear, devoid of self-seeking, an embodied theory. The materialist conception of history is his life-blood. He resembles a professor in his desire to have the theory understood & in his fury with those who misunderstand or disagree; also in his love of expounding. I put three questions to him. (1) I asked whether & how far he recognized the peculiarity of English conditions. The answer was unsatisfactory to me. He admits that there is little chance of revolution now, & that the working man is not yet disgusted with Parliamentary government. He hopes this result may be brought about by a Labour Ministry, particularly if Henderson is premier. But when I suggested that whatever is possible in England may occur without bloodshed, he waved aside the suggestion as fantastic. I got little impression of knowledge or psychological imagination.
(2) I asked him whether he thought it possible to establish communism firmly & fully in a country containing such a large majority of peasants. He admitted it was difficult. He laughed over the exchange the peasant is compelled to make, of food for paper — the worthlessness of Russian paper struck him as comic. But he said things would right themselves when there are goods to offer to the peasant. For this he looks partly to electrification in industry, which he says is a technical necessity in Russia; (& will take 10 years) but chiefly he looks to the raising of the blockade. He described the division between rich & poor peasants, & the

He said that as late as July 1917 the Bolsheviks were not only persecuted, but even assaulted by the Moscow mob. He said that very few understand the theory of the govt, but that many support it out of instinct. I got the impression that he despises the populace & is an intellectual aristocrat.

very much', Russell said years later. 'Bolshevism', went his verdict in a letter to Ottoline, 'is a close tyrannical bureaucracy with a spy system more elaborate and terrible than the Tsar's, and an aristocracy as insolent and unfeeling, composed of Americanized Jews.'

Detestation of Bolshevism was to influence Russell's fortunes at more than one point during the next few years. As the bitterness of the war years slowly evaporated, many who had opposed it were able to achieve positions of power or influence. Clifford Allen was raised to the peerage and MacDonald became Prime Minister. There were many other less important examples. In general, such men turned a kindly eye on the Soviet Union; but Russell, damned for his pacifist views in the conservative demonology, was put beyond the pale by potential Left-wing supporters for hammering home his observation that under Bolshevism, 'no vestige of liberty remains, in thought or speech or action'. Two decades later, as the Russians engulfed eastern Europe, these views which had ruled out his use as a propagandist in the Second World War chimed in well with conventional wisdom, and helped bring him back into respectability, a potential leader in the anti-Russian cause.

In the summer of 1920 Russell had to cope with different problems. Dora Black had courageously gone to Russia under her own steam but she and Russell had not met there, for reasons beyond their control. It was probably all to the good. To Colette, who had been waiting for him on his return, Russell wrote that Dora 'loved the Bolshies' as fervently as Clifford Allen still did, and that he was thinking of breaking with her. The idea was eventually abandoned after some weeks of emotional gyrations during which Russell at last resolved to organize a divorce from Alys: in the process he obtained the necessary incriminating evidence, first with Colette, then with Dora — somewhat resembling the over-cautious who wear both belt and braces.

The catalyst for this flurry of sudden activity had been a letter Russell had found waiting for him on returning from Russia. It came from the Chinese Lecture Association and asked whether he would give a year's course in Peking University. He decided, in principle, that he would go, but it would mean leaving Colette, unwilling to abandon her career. For Russell the problem was resolved when he discovered that Dora was willing to come to China with him. Meanwhile, he continued to stress to Colette how terrible the long parting from her would be, and how much he loved her. With Trinity, he for the moment kept his options open, successfully asking in July for a year's leave of absence.

In August, Russell and Dora Black left for China, travelling to Paris and then Marseilles before sailing to Shanghai. In Paris Russell finished *The Practice and Theory of Bolshevism*. 'I expect universal abuse but that won't do the book any harm in the long run', he had warned Stanley Unwin, a prophecy that was correct on both points; the book was praised by people he hated, such as Winston Churchill and

A page from Russell's diary for May 1920, in which he describes his hour-long interview with Lenin. 'Nothing in his manner or bearing suggests the man who has power. He looks at his visitor very close, & screws up one eye. He laughs a great deal; at first his laugh seems merely friendly & jolly, but gradually one finds it grim. He is dictatorial, calm, incapable of fear, devoid of self-seeking, an embodied theory.'

Lloyd George, but denigrated by many friends to whom Russell had now become a renegade.

In Peking Russell burned his boats with Trinity, writing to the Master, J. J. Thomson, and regretfully resigning his lectureship. Then he and Dora Black began a life that both enjoyed. He gave 'official' lectures on mathematical logic, the analysis of matter, the analysis of mind, and similar subjects; unofficially he lectured on relativity and gravitation and found time to address and help small study-groups and seminars. Miss Black lectured on social subjects and politics. Both were interested in Chinese life, in the future of a country just creeping into industrialization, and in the beauties of a landscape neither had previously seen.

The freshness soon began to wear off. 'We are both very happy here, but', Russell wrote to Ottoline before the end of February 1921, 'one couldn't stay here for ever unless one were prepared to retire from the world. It is not here that important things begin.' Whether or not Russell would have cut short the visit because of home-sickness and political isolation no one can say. But the issue was decided by an event in mid-March. Lecturing in a school a hundred miles south of Peking, Russell began to feel cold. The return was delayed by a series of mishaps and outside the city walls there was a further hour's wait before the gates could be opened. By this time he was running a high temperature, and in the city's German Hospital double pneumonia was diagnosed.

For a while he seemed unlikely to survive, and his death was reported in Japan where he planned to lecture on leaving Peking. Russell himself later quoted a missionary as having said: 'Missionaries may be pardoned for heaving a sigh of relief at the news of Mr. Bertrand Russell's death.' Hearing the news in London, Frank Russell thought his brother's death improbable. 'First', he wrote to Russell, 'because you wouldn't do such a thing, secondly because you weren't in Japan, thirdly because you hadn't told me and fourthly because if the news came from America there was a *prima facie* assumption that it was untrue.'

By the end of April Russell was recovering. Some weeks later he learned that Dora was pregnant, a fact that increased the wish to get back to England as soon as possible. They finally left in July, travelling via Japan and the United States and arriving in London on August 27. Alys had been granted a decree *nisi* in May; six months normally passed before a decree was made absolute, and since Dora was due to give birth in November, the legitimacy of the potential fourth earl would clearly be a close-run thing. But Alys supported an application that the process should be speeded-up, the papers came through on 21 September, and Russell was able to remarry six days later.

Alys was for the time being to be expunged not only from his life but, as far as was possible, from the record. To Colette, still his beloved as he had told her following his recovery in Peking, but now

John Francis Stanley Russell, the 2nd Earl and Russell's elder brother, usually known as Frank.

Opposite: Russell and Dora Black arriving in Peking in 1920. They soon moved into a single-storey house built round a courtyard in the eastern part of the city. 'We have old wiggly Chinese bookshelves, heavy black Chinese chairs, a big divan of the sort they used to use for smoking opium,' Russell wrote to Lady Ottoline; 'lovely square tables, all black. . . . Our Chinese friends are amazed at our not wanting European rubbish!'

Russell and (seated) his wife Dora during his campaign as a Labour Candidate for Chelsea in the Parliamentary election of 1922. He failed to oust the sitting Conservative Member, Sir Samuel Hoare, and failed again in 1923. His wife did the same when she stood as a candidate in 1924.

regretfully if satisfactorily discarded, he explained the situation in a brief final meeting. 'In the autumn of 1921', she wrote a decade later, 'there was an epidemic of marriage. B.R. was the first to go down.'

Russell now began to earn his living in London, as author, educator, and propagandist for the causes in which he believed. It was not an easy task. The notoriety which he had achieved in the war was still remembered, and it was significant that when he tried to rent a house in Chelsea landlords were unwilling to have him as a tenant. Eventually he bought a house there, and stood unsuccessfully as a Labour candidate in the constituency in 1922 and 1923. Dora had no better luck in 1924.

It was only in 1926 that Trinity invited him to give the Tarner Lectures, and with this exception the academic establishment tended to avoid him. He was thus kept financially afloat only by his facility for writing immaculate prose, at a high speed, on any required subject. Between 1922 and 1927 he produced *The Problem of China* – his own choice of title had been *The White Peril* – *The ABC of Atoms, Icarus, or the Future of Science, What I Believe, The ABC of Relativity, On Education* and *An Outline of Philosophy*, as well as *The Analysis of Matter*. At times he was hard-pressed, deploring in March 1925 that he 'must write 50,000 words before May 1st'. To the National Secular Society he gave one of his most famous lectures, 'Why I Am Not a Christian'. And to journals and newspapers in both Britain and the United States he wrote on whatever subject was commissioned.

His survival in the bleak and tough world of popular writing was helped by the long periods he could spend at Carn Voel, an isolated house within a few miles of Land's End which he had bought soon after settling in London. Russell had a strong attachment to the mountains and an attachment to the sea which was only slightly less strong. Carn Voel, with strong Channel breakers at the front and the Pendeen moors at the back, almost filled the bill. Here his son John and his daughter Kate, who had been born two years after John, were able to enjoy what was in some ways an idyllic existence.

The months spent at Carn Voel during the mid-1920s were among the happiest in Russell's life. There was as yet no hint of a break with Dora. He had two fine children and he was bringing them up in an environment which ideally suited his tastes. He was writing as fluently as ever, and if work had not brought him a fortune he was recovering from the impecunious embarrassments of the war. Indeed, his daughter remembers in their Cornwall home a cook, housemaid, gardener, a man to drive the car and nanny or governess.

'The beauty of the Cornish coast', Russell wrote years later, 'is inextricably mixed in my memories with the ecstasy of watching two healthy happy children learning the joys of sea and rocks and sun and storm.' But it was not only his own children who fascinated him as much as they were fascinated by him. There was not only a regular stream of adult visitors to Carn Voel but many companions for John and Kate, some of whom would stay the whole summer. For all, he had an apparently bottomless fund of stories, of adventures that he knew could be sought on the beaches or the moors behind, of exciting revelations that could be found if only you were shown where to look for them. Thus his cherished gold watch – almost certainly Lord John's – was often brought into play. 'For babies', says his daughter, 'he would hold it by the chain and swing it gently, solemnly intoning "Tick-tock, tick-tock", as their eyes moved to and fro. Older children were shown the face and the winding mechanism, sometimes even the works within the inmost door. Those who were really careful were even allowed to open it themselves, pressing the little levers that made the golden doors spring open.'

In 1927 Russell added to his responsibilities by starting Beacon Hill School, a courageous enterprise which soon received more notoriety than it deserved. Dora Russell has pointed out that the school was started as a joint enterprise with her husband, and that while Russell opted out following their divorce, the school continued under her control and management for roughly another decade.

Both parents wanted their children to be educated along the progressive lines of which they approved. No existing school appeared to fill the bill and the obvious solution was to create their own. The first problem, that of finding a suitable building, was solved by Frank Russell, deep in financial trouble and glad to lease Telegraph House, his home high on the Sussex Downs. Beacon Hill School, named after the nearby point from which the news of Trafalgar had been received and transmitted by heliograph on its way from Portsmouth to London, opened on 22 September 1927, with twelve boarders and five day children.

Isolated Carn Voel, a house
standing back from the south
Cornish coast near Porthcurno.
'It is lovely here,' Russell told
Ottoline, ' – the birds sing all day
– there are larks & thrushes &
blackbirds & cuckoos & curlews
& seagulls all round the house &
ships sail by, & at night one
hears the sea in the distance
booming on the rocks, & there is
blackthorn & whitethorn, &
bluebells & buttercups, & green
fields & gorse moors, all without
stirring from the house.' *Right:*
Russell with one of his children
bathing off Porthcurno.

Russell and Dora with their two children, John and Kate, taken in 1927, probably on the beach near Carn Voel; and, again in the late 1920s, on the south coast of Cornwall. Here, Russell wrote, John had 'the advantages of playing on the sands, then boating, then climbing on the rocks, & all the splendour of the sea, which is a good thing to have in one's memories of childhood.'

Telegraph House, rented by Russell from his brother for use as Beacon Hill School. Built by Frank Russell on the top of the Sussex Downs, it occupied the site of an Admiralty semaphore station, one of the chain by which the news of Trafalgar was sent from Portsmouth to London.

Its character was suggested in a letter Russell wrote to one prospective parent:

With regard to religion there is no religious teaching of any sort or kind. The children learn about the various religions of the world as historical facts but no one religion is treated differently from any other. A good deal of trouble is taken to make the education such as will not inspire patriotism, more particularly in the teaching of history and geography which I do personally. As for teaching the brotherhood of man I have the same objection that I have to explicit moral instruction in that it tends to produce either hypocrisy or rebellion. Morality must grow, it cannot be implanted by precept.

These ideas were not overwhelmingly popular in Britain fifty years ago. It also became known that, as Dora Russell herself said, the children were allowed to remove all their clothes in the summer if they wished to, especially for outdoor dancing and exercise, another practice which made Beacon Hill a target for popular criticism. Yet Beacon Hill, judging by the record, and by the reminiscences of those who worked there, was not the caricature sometimes described in the press. But neither was it entirely the successful venture that its supporters still maintain. One reason was that the children in no sense formed a typical cross-section on which the Russells' educational ideas could be fairly tested. Secondly, there was insufficient money for the job, and Russell was driven to ask parents if they would help 'by paying fees more nearly proportional to the cost'. Perhaps more important were the limitations of Russell himself. A school, he was later to write, 'is an administrative enterprise and I found myself deficient in skill as an administrator'. Indeed, he had at times a singular helplessness, a legacy of the Pembroke Lodge days when contact with the servants' bell solved all such problems.

The need to finance the school kept Russell hard at work for the first years of its existence. His literary versatility was demonstrated in what appeared to be an endless cascade of articles for almost anyone who would pay handsomely: *The Daily Express, Harper's, Atlantic Monthly*, and the *Jewish Daily Forward* were all served with his articles, many produced in the top room of Beacon Hill's uniquely ugly tower.

He tried to work only in the morning, but was not content with an output of less than 3,000 words, usually dictated to a secretary as fast as she could take them down. If that quota was not filled by the end of

Russell and his wife Dora with some of the children at Beacon Hill School.

the morning, he worked on after lunch. 'I plan it all out in my head beforehand', he explained to a visitor in 1930, 'so that before I start it it's all finished. I used to make elaborate notes because I couldn't hold as much in my head as I can now. When I have a book to write of 60,000 words, I start twenty days before it is due at the publishers. If I can only work two days a week, that is, when I go to London, then it takes me ten weeks.'

He was writing only for money, and frankly admitted that he did not mind pot-boiling, adding on one occasion: 'I have no "lofty feelings".' He believed himself to be past creative work, sometimes telling visitors that he was too old. As for mathematics and philosophy, he could say: 'No good work is done after forty, or perhaps I should say thirty-five. I believe that experience of life and knowledge of men is inimical to the intellect. Human experience rubs down the edge of the mind. It should be as hard as a diamond. But the more you use it to cut through ordinary life the more blunt it becomes.'

Russell's words on pot-boiling should not be taken too literally. Although much of his output during the Beacon Hill years can correctly be called 'popular', a good deal of it expounded the social and political ideas in which he believed. The same combination of spreading his own gospel and raising money for Beacon Hill was true of his four American tours, made in 1924, 1927, 1929 and 1931. Russell records returning home from one of them with 10,000 dollars profit from a two-month tour; the others appear to have been equally successful. However, not only did the proceeds help to keep the school financially afloat but the lectures themselves made American audiences aware of the radical views on education, politics, and marriage and divorce which were spreading in Britain.

In the American visits of 1896 and 1914 he had spoken only on mathematics and philosophy; and even though some listeners had noted his unusual views on other subjects, it had been as a lecturer on purely academic matters that he had been assessed. When, during the war, he had written in American journals on current affairs, he had been mainly concerned with the war with the Central Powers, a subject on which many readers for long held no very firm views. Russell had remained acceptable.

In 1924, and during the three following tours, he spoke to audiences which he knew would have little liking for what he had to say about either politics or social questions. However, he made no attempt to dissimulate, and told his listeners that if world government ever came it would be by means of American imperialism. Many no doubt agreed, until he went on to add: 'The empire of American finance will be in the highest degree illiberal and cruel. It will crush trade unionism, control education, encourage competition among workers while avoiding it among the capitalists. It will make life everywhere ugly, uniform, laborious and monotonous.' But if he thus offended the Right, his views on Russia, proclaimed as vehemently as they had been in *The Practice and Theory of Bolshevism*, offended the Left.

. . . the only one Mr Russell gives is that it is only nature-after-all.

An American reaction to *Marriage and Morals*.

But it was not so much Russell's political views which set the scene for his later unhappy wartime years in America. In his second tour he spoke on 'Companionate Marriage' and before he returned for the third tour he had written *Marriage and Morals*. Although neither was particularly unconventional, even in the 1920s, and even though he came down heavily in support of marriage, they were enough to arouse Bishop Manning of the Protestant Episcopal Church and, through him, much of America's Catholic population. The philosopher-mathematician, who although not wearing a halo had at least been religiously neutral, had now sprouted horns. The outcome was that when Russell returned to Britain in December 1931 after tours that had taken him from New York to San Francisco, his standing in the United States had become very similar to what it already was in Britain. In his own field he was the Bertrand Russell of *Principia Mathematica* and the other works that had given him an honoured place; outside it, he had become for many the 'aggressive propagandist against both Christian faith and Christian morality', the man to whom few fathers would willingly introduce a daughter. By 1931 Russell had reached in America much the same position that Sigmund Freud had reached in Vienna at the turn of the century.

Yet whatever the Americans – or many of the British for that matter – might think of him, Russell still occupied a unique position in his own field even though he had not held an academic post for more than a decade. And when Wittgenstein returned to England in 1929 and applied for a PhD at Cambridge based on the *Tractatus*, it was Russell who was asked by Trinity to examine him. The occasion had a mild air of farce. First Russell and Moore chatted with Wittgenstein as an old friend. Neither appeared ready to start the examination and eventually Russell had to exhort Moore: 'Go on, you've got to ask him some questions – you're the Professor.' There was a brief and inconclusive discussion. The viva suddenly ended as Wittgenstein got up, slapped his examiners on the shoulders and told them: 'Don't worry, I know you'll *never* understand it.'

In 1931 Frank died and Russell became the 3rd Earl, an elevation for which he had no particular taste. Although he informed the chief Labour Whip in the House of Lords that he would take his seat, and would vote Labour, he had no intention of abandoning writing which he considered to be his proper job. As for the title, that was, he told his American publisher, a great nuisance and he would not use it. This was a great relief to some of his acquaintances in America; one had asked Whitehead, now a professor at Harvard, how he should now address Russell, only to be told: 'I always call him Bertie.'

The new Earl was by this time not only a newsworthy figure, the typical English 'character'. He was also a man whom the literary world could recognize with little difficulty in the works of those who had observed him at Garsington Manor. Among the first portraits was D. H. Lawrence's Sir Joshua Malleson of *Women in Love*: 'an elderly sociologist . . . a learned dry Baronet of fifty who was always making witticisms and laughing at them heartily in a harsh horse-laugh.' The figure was redrawn as Bertie Reid in Lawrence's 'The Blind Man' – 'a little dark man, with a very big forehead, thin, wispy hair, and sad, large eyes.' Gilbert Cannan had Russell as Melian Stokes, the don in three of his novels, *Pugs and Peacocks*, *Sembal* and *The House of Prophecy*. In Siegfried Sassoon's *Memoirs of an Infantry Officer*, Russell is the Thornton Tyrrell who, as in real life, encouraged Sassoon to make his famous statement of disobedience as a serving officer in the First World War. And in Eliot's 'Prufrock', Mr Apollinax catches just that hint of the satyr which with Russell was rarely far below the surface.

If it was to be left to Constance Malleson to give, in *The Coming Back*, an almost undisguised picture of Russell – as well as of Lady Ottoline and her husband; Clifford Allen; T. S. Eliot and Dr Joad – the portrait which distressed Russell most was Aldous Huxley's Mr Scogan in *Crome Yellow*. But while Huxley described his Scogan/Russell as 'like one of those extinct bird-lizards of the Tertiary' he also provided his fictional character with a not-too-inaccurate summary of Russell's views:

If you're to do anything reasonable in this world, you must have a class of people who are secure, safe from public opinion, safe from poverty, leisured, not compelled to waste their time in the imbecile routines that go by the name of Honest Work. You must have a class of which the members can think and, within the obvious limits, do what they please. You must have a class in which people who have eccentricities can indulge them and in which eccentricity in general will be tolerated and understood. That's the important thing about an aristocracy.

Russell and G. E. Moore, photographed by Moore's wife about 1941 in Princeton. Some years earlier Russell and Moore had examined Wittgenstein for a PhD based on the *Tractatus*.

Russell's accession to the earldom brought him into the public eye once more, and it was inevitable that when his marriage with Dora broke up in the 1930s the complex divorce case would receive maximum publicity. The first test of the marriage had come on his return from the American lecture tour in 1924 during which he had had a brief *affaire* of which he told his wife. They had already agreed that such *affaires* should be tolerated on either side and it was only, as Russell later wrote, that 'in later years things increasingly went wrong'.

The statement was no exaggeration. When, in February 1935, Dora Russell was granted a decree *nisi* in London, the President of the Court noted that:

> her statement shows that both instances of her adultery of which she had spoken were preceded by at least two cases of infidelity on the part of her husband, and that he had been guilty of numerous acts of adultery in circumstances which are usually held to aggravate the offence. I am referring to the fact that she spoke of the infidelity of the respondent with persons in the household or engaged in the business in which they were mutually occupied.

The following year, 1936, Russell married for the third time. His bride was Patricia Spence, usually known as 'Peter'. A woman many years younger than himself, she had been employed by the Russells as a governess in 1930 while an Oxford undergraduate, had become a favourite of the two children, and had already helped him in his writings. Of *Freedom and Organization, 1814–1914* Russell recorded that

Peter had done 'half the research, a large part of the planning, and small portions of the actual writing besides making innumerable valuable suggestions'. She did much of the research for *The Amberley Papers* in which she and Russell chronicled the history of his family, and helped in preparing *Power: A New Social Analysis*.

After the divorce Dora moved the school from Telegraph House and Russell and his new wife moved in. But he was once again hard pressed for money and before the end of 1937 was forced to sell the estate which his brother had bought at the end of the century. Then he was invited to give at Oxford a series of lectures on 'Words and Facts', and moved to a house in Kidlington, a few miles from the city. In the autumn of 1938 he moved to the United States.

Two years earlier Russell had explained to his American publisher, Warder Norton, that he had three reasons for wishing to leave England. He had a lot of ideas which he thought were important and wanted to work out. Although he did not emphasize the fact to Norton, this would be difficult without some academic post, and he seemed unlikely to secure one in Britain. He was, in any case, faced with what he called the likelihood of such poverty as would prevent him from giving a proper education to Conrad, the child of his

Russell and his youngest son, Conrad Sebastian Robert, photographed soon after Russell's arrival in Chicago in 1938.

Russell's third wife, Patricia (Peter) Spence. She was to play a significant part in the events which later brought him back to Trinity.

marriage to Peter. Finally, he did not consider Europe a fit place for children since war seemed to be imminent and England was likely to suffer most in it.

To Moore in Cambridge he explained that he had legally to pay between £800 and £900 a year to dependents but had an unearned income of only £300. Was there, he wondered, the chance of a post in Cambridge? Moore appears to have been unwilling to help, and Russell then turned to Whitehead, now approaching retirement from the Harvard post he had taken up in 1924. Russell suggested that he himself might be a suitable successor. But Harvard was not interested. The chances appeared to be better at Princeton's Institute for Advanced Study, and Einstein, Oscar Veblen and Herman Weyl, the Director's advisers in mathematics and philosophy, were agreeable that Russell should join them. But the Director was Abraham Flexner. His brother and confidante was Simon, husband of Helen

Thomas, cousin of Alys and a member of the Quaker community which had been dismayed at Russell's abandonment of his first wife. Abraham Flexner vetoed the appointment. Eventually the University of Chicago invited Russell to give a series of lectures during the academic year 1938–39 as Visiting Professor of Philosophy.

He sailed for the United States with his family as the Munich crisis was rising to what was for Britain its humiliating climax. He returned to Britain in the summer of 1944. In between, there lay six years of misfortune, qualified only by the fact that during that time he wrote *A History of Western Philosophy*, a best-seller that was to bring great financial reward during the early post-war years.

At first, all went well. He disliked Chicago but liked the University, and would have been happy if his contract had been renewed. Renewal failed to come. In the spring of 1939 there arrived, instead, the offer of a three-year contract with the University of California. Russell quickly accepted and the late summer of 1939 found him in Santa Barbara with Peter and Conrad, eagerly awaiting the arrival of Kate and John. It had been agreed that they should visit their father for the holidays; and it had been tacitly agreed that if war broke out they would not return to Britain until it was over.

In theory, this was exactly what Russell wanted. But after 3 September 1939, and increasingly as the threat to Britain grew and the night bombing blitz began to ravage Britain's cities, Russell's

Russell, his third wife Peter, his daughter Kate (far left) and his elder son John (far right) at Yosemite in the summer of 1939. The children had recently arrived from Britain and Russell took them for a visit to the High Sierra Camps, 9,000 ft up in Yosemite National Park. By the time they all returned to Santa Barbara the Second World War had started.

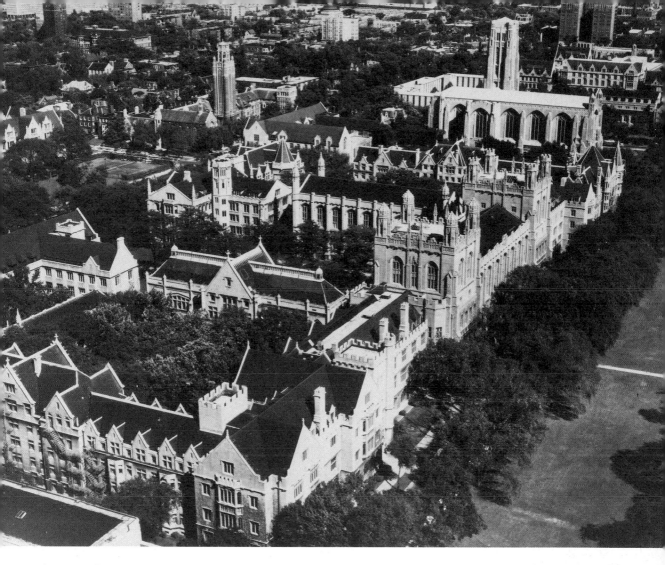

views on the war and on his position – 3,000 miles from the action – began to change.

In 1936 he had published *Which Way to Peace?*, a book in which he had argued that the horrors of bombing would be greater than those of submission to the Germans. This belief survived the Munich Pact and even the occupation of Czechoslovakia in March 1939. But once war had begun his position began to change, and it changed with increasing speed as the prospects of invasion grew. The innate love of Britain was soon swamping pacifist ideals and in June 1940 he felt forced to say so to Kingsley Martin, hoping that Martin would make his position clear in the columns of *The New Statesman*. Then, curiously echoing Einstein who in 1933 had renounced his pacifism and said he would fight against Hitler had he been younger, Russell added: 'If I were young enough to fight myself, I should do so, but it is more difficult to urge others.'

Chicago University, where in late 1938 and early 1939 Russell gave an undergraduate course on 'The Problems of Philosophy', ran a graduate seminar on semantics, and delivered a series of lectures based on his book *Power*.

This apostasy at first seems curious since even in 1936 Russell must have realized what German occupation would mean. However, there was, as usual, a logical reason for his change of heart. Two decades previously, in 'The Ethics of War', he had soberly outlined how various factors should be balanced to decide whether any particular war was justifiable or not. And by June 1940 the situation was different in one important way from that of 1936. 'Stalin's Russia has turned against us', he told Gilbert Murray. 'I have no doubt that the Soviet Government is even worse than Hitler's, and it will be a misfortune if it survives.' In the First World War, H. G. Wells had probably shocked Russell with his declaration that 'Every sword that is drawn against Germany is now a sword of peace'. In 1940 Russell's patriotism was supported by the thought that every arm raised against Germany appeared to be raised against the Soviet system as well.

The feeling, which developed logically from his experiences of 1920, was to be a handicap after the German invasion of Russia in the summer of 1941 had turned an enemy into an ally overnight. More than once after 1941 Russell was to find himself looking for work in America. More than once there were official hints and soundings-out to discover whether such an accomplished speaker might not be used to expound the British cause in America. But fear of what Russell might say about such strange bed-fellows as Britain and Soviet Russia stopped them all.

More than a year before the transformation of the war in mid-1941, Russell had been at the centre of a notorious legal case. He had liked California more than he liked Chicago, but he disliked President Sproul of the University of California even more than he had disliked President Hutchins of Chicago. Thus when he received the offer of a Chair from the College of the City of New York in February 1940, he resigned from his three-year appointment in California. Only later did he realize that the New York offer was not yet ratified and that his precipitate action might leave him, once again, without a job. Sproul accepted the resignation quickly and refused to consider any withdrawal. Russell now found himself at the mercy of a religiously inspired campaign which maintained that he was the last possible man to help lead young Americans towards the second half of the twentieth century.

The case which developed has, in today's climate, the makings of farce, but forty years ago it represented a serious attack on academic freedom which, as *The New York Times* stated, 'struck at the security and intellectual independence of every faculty member in every public college and university in the United States'.

Russell had been hired to teach logic, certain problems in the foundations of mathematics, and the relationship between the pure and the applied sciences to all-male classes. It would have been difficult for anyone to find much sexual titillation in such subjects and on 18 March the New York Board of Higher Education voted to

"THE CHAIR OF INDECENCY"

In 1940, the New York Supreme Court ordered the New York Board of Higher Education to rescind Russell's appointment to a Chair in the College of the City of New York. During the hearing, Justice McGeehan claimed that Russell's appointment would 'in effect [be] establishing a chair of indecency'. This *New York Times* cartoon was one by-product.

confirm his appointment. However, the author of *Marriage and Morals* was not to win so easily, and the following day a Mrs Jean Kay sought a state Supreme Court order directing the College to revoke the appointment. Among her grounds was her fear of what would happen to her young daughter were she taught by Russell, the fact that this was impossible appearing to be irrelevant. The Supreme Court decided that the appointment should be revoked.

To understand what today appears to be an extraordinary verdict it is necessary to consider how Russell was then viewed by a sizeable percentage of the American public. Today, he is most likely to be denigrated for his attitude to the Vietnamese war, for his post-1954 opposition to nuclear weapons or for his earlier support for their use, if need be, against Stalinist Russia. In 1940, opposition was based almost exclusively on his advocacy of an unconventional sexual morality and on his atheism. To *The Tablet* he was 'the philosophical

AN INQUIRY
INTO
MEANING AND
TRUTH

BY

BERTRAND RUSSELL

M.A., F.R.S.

Holder of the Nicholas Murray Butler Medal of Columbia
University (1915), the Sylvester Medal of the Royal Society
(1932) and the de Morgan Medal of the London Mathematical Society (1933). Honorary Member of the Reale
Accademia dei Lincei. Fellow (1895–1901) and Lecturer
(1910–1916) of Trinity College, Cambridge. Herbert
Spencer Lecturer at Oxford (1914). Visiting Professor
of Philosophy at Harvard University (1914) and at The
Chinese Government University of Peking (1920–1921).
Tarner Lecturer at Cambridge (1926). Special Lecturer
at the London School of Economics and Political Science
(1937) and at The University of Oxford (1938). Visiting
Professor of Philosophy at the University of Chicago
(1938–1939). Professor of Philosophy at the University of
California at Los Angeles (1939–1940). Occasional Lecturer
at the Universities of Uppsala, Copenhagen, Barcelona, the
Sorbonne, etc., etc.

Judicially pronounced unworthy to be Professor of Philosophy at the College of the City of New York (1940)

LONDON
GEORGE ALLEN AND UNWIN LTD

anarchist and moral nihilist of Great Britain'; to the Jesuit *American*, he was the 'dessicated, divorced, and decadent advocate of sexual promiscuity'. A telegram to La Guardia, the Mayor of New York, after warning that 'Quicksands threaten! The snake is in the grass! The worm is busy in the mind', implored the mayor to protect students 'from the baneful influence of him of the poisoned pen – an ape of genius, the devil's minister of men'. Even this paled against the claim made in court by Mrs Kay's lawyer, who maintained that Russell was 'lecherous, libidinous, lustful, venerous, erotomaniac, aphrodisiac, irreverent, narrow-minded, untruthful, and bereft of moral fibre'.

As Americans, John Dewey later remarked of the court verdict, 'we can only blush with shame for this scar on our repute for fair play'. In practical terms, Russell was out of a job; he was due to give the William James lectures at Harvard in September, but while preparing them feared he might have to send his wife and children back to Britain. Harvard, as might be expected, refused to be drawn into the witch-hunt and Russell gave the lectures as planned. When they were published as *An Inquiry into Meaning and Truth*, he was able to prepare a unique title-page. It carried a seventeen-line list of his honours followed by a final item: 'Judicially pronounced unworthy to be Professor of Philosophy at the College of the City of New York (1940).' But the page was printed only in the British edition.

It was not only the Harvard lectures which helped restore Russell's jauntiness. Dr Albert Barnes, the individualistic if eccentric founder and director of the Barnes Foundation at Merion, outside Philadelphia, had decided to broaden his course in aesthetics to include the philosophical and social background of art. Who better to do this than the attacked Bertrand Russell? By the end of 1940 Russell had signed a five-year contract with Barnes, had moved from California to a 200-year-old farmhouse thirty miles from Philadelphia, and could look forward to the prospect of pleasant and well-paid work.

Once again, he was to be disillusioned. A series of bickering disputes with Barnes culminated, after two years, in his illegal dismissal. He was eventually to win his case against Barnes, but this was to take almost two years. Meanwhile, as he wrote to Stanley Unwin, he had lost his 'whole income (illegally) at three days notice' and was once again out of a job. British currency restrictions prevented any money being sent to him across the Atlantic and the first months of 1943 were among the most financially desperate of his life.

Then the tide began to turn. He was invited privately to Bryn Mawr where he stayed with Lucy Donnelly and renewed his acquaintance with her friend Edith Finch. The Philosophy Department received an anonymous gift so that Russell could be paid for a series of lectures on the Postulates of Scientific Method. Next, he was invited to lecture at Princeton, an academic Mecca which had already drawn Albert Einstein, Kurt Gödel and Wolfgang Pauli. A substantial advance payment came from Simon & Schuster for American

Opposite: The cancellation of Russell's appointment to a Chair at the College of the City of New York came some months before his William James lectures at Harvard were published as *An Inquiry into Meaning and Truth*. In the English edition the list of his qualifications was concluded with the words: 'Judicially pronounced unworthy to be Professor of Philosophy at the College of the City of New York (1940)'.

Edith Finch, Russell's fourth wife, photographed in 1927. She had met Russell at Bryn Mawr, where both she and their mutual friend Lucy Donnelly were on the staff. They were married after Peter had divorced him for desertion in 1952.

rights in the Barnes lectures which Russell was already turning into the money-spinning *History of Western Philosophy*. Eventually the case against Barnes was settled in his favour with the award of 20,000 dollars.

Finally there came the best news of all. Once again he was invited back to Trinity. The available details of how this happened are complicated and incomplete. But Peter had written a note on the attitude of the anti-Russell groups in America which had been read to the members of Trinity Council. Vera Brittain and her husband, who had met Russell in California, triggered off a quite separate lobbying for Russell's return which was organized by C. D. Broad. And the ground had been prepared by G. H. Hardy's brief pamphlet, 'Bertrand Russell and Trinity', which left no doubt that there was a wrong waiting to be righted.

The day that Trinity's offer of a fellowship arrived was one of the happiest days in Russell's life. Within a few weeks, as Allied troops struggled to maintain their toehold in the deep and bloody *bocage* of Normandy, he recrossed the Atlantic. Half a century before, returning from Paris, he had kissed the English earth on landing. Now, once he had again settled in to Cambridge, he could write to Lucy Donnelly that 'all this is such a change from the unspeakable misery we endured in America that one feels intoxicated'.

Back in Trinity, Russell was delighted to be allocated Newton's rooms. But he wanted a home once more and was glad when arrival

G. H. Hardy, whose 'Bertrand Russell and Trinity' left little doubt that Russell's dismissal from his Lectureship in 1916 had been unjust. He played an important role in organizing Russell's return in 1944.

Opposite: Russell in a corner of Neville's Court, Trinity, in 1945. He was overjoyed at being back, and particularly in having been given Newton's rooms. 'I dine in hall and enjoy seeing dons I used to know 30 years ago,' he wrote to Colette. 'George Trevy [George Trevelyan, then Master of Trinity] is much mellowed, very friendly & nice. One can still play the game of great-uncles with him & his wife – his was Macaulay, hers Matthew Arnold, & the only subject they disagree about is which was the greater.'

of the 20,000 dollars from the Barnes Foundation allowed him to buy a house in the town. Here he could settle down once again with Peter and Conrad who had followed him across the Atlantic.

His fellowship did not require that he teach, or give lectures, but he did both, one of his annual courses evolving into *Human Knowledge: Its Scope and Limits*, his last survey of the problems associated with an empiricist philosophy. He was popular with students, an ornament to Trinity, and one of the sights of the town. Dining in hall, he enjoyed seeing dons he had known thirty years earlier and as far as professional work was concerned there was only one niggling worry. This was provided by Wittgenstein, now the successor to Moore in the chair of philosophy: he had by this time abandoned the ideas of the *Tractatus* for those of a new linguistic philosophy outlined in his posthumous *Philosophical Investigations*. Russell was allergic to Wittgenstein's new views and there was at least one confrontation which rumour quickly – and incorrectly – expanded into a quarrel among dons so violent that the now eminent Wittgenstein had used a poker to threaten a Russell supporter.

Russell, his third wife Peter and his younger son Conrad, in Cambridge about 1947. He was an extremely popular lecturer. 'The things you would remember after the lecture', wrote one student, 'were the animated sparkle of his eyes and the quick decisive movements that showed nothing of the palsy of old age; also, and chiefly, the virility of his mind and senses.'

George Trevelyan, Master of Trinity, in the Library. Walking past the marble busts, Russell remarked to a friend, 'I shall be here one day.'

The speed with which any anecdote about Russell travelled through Cambridge was an index of his fame not only as a philosopher but also as a public figure of somewhat unnerving authority. If it was natural that Trinity should accept Russell back into the fold, not only acknowledging his position but doing its collegial best to make restitution for its action in 1915, the attitude of authority in general was at first glance more curious. Between 1945 and 1954 Russell became a regular broadcaster for the BBC and was awarded the honour of delivering the Corporation's first series of Reith Lectures, an honour which might have made that noble lord turn in his retirement. He addressed the Royal Empire Society and he lectured to the Imperial Defence College for a number of years. He lectured for the British Council in Belgium and Switzerland, as well as to the troops in blockaded Berlin, and in Norway where he had a remarkable escape from death. The flying-boat in which he was flown from Oslo to Trondheim for an official lecture sank on landing and Russell, aged 76, found himself swimming to safety in the icy northern waters.

Russell in bed in Trondheim after swimming to safety from a flying-boat which crashed there in 1948 while taking him to lecture on behalf of the British Council. Asked how he felt while swimming for his life in northern waters, he replied with the one word: 'Cold'.

The Order of Merit, conferred on Russell in 1949. Bestowing it, George VI, affable but slightly embarrassed at decorating an ex-jailbird, commented: 'You have sometimes behaved in a way which would not do if generally adopted.' Russell claimed that the reply, 'Like your brother', sprang to his mind.

Nineteen passengers died in the plane; Russell survived without injury and despite cancellation of his official lecture spoke informally to the students of Trondheim University.

In 1949 the Order of Merit was conferred on him, an honour restricted to only twenty-four British members, and a handful of foreign honorary members. This ultimate recognition that Bertie was not the apotheosis of the anti-Christ was partly due to a change in the tide of opinion which made it increasingly difficult to regard his views on sex and society with quite the horror of pre-war years. Yet his long detestation of Communism could not be ignored and, in the immediate post-war period, neither could his views on what should be done before Russia acquired nuclear weapons. His extreme left-wing supporters have long wriggled on the hook of his published statements – even maintaining that while he advocated the threat of nuclear weapons against Russia he did not advocate their use. But the inescapable facts are that within ten weeks of Hiroshima, Russell was emphasizing the dangers of giving nuclear information to Russia and adding: 'I should, for my part, prefer all the chaos and destruction of a war conducted by means of the atomic bomb to the universal domination of a government having the evil characteristics of the Nazis.' And if the USSR refused to join a world Confederation, then, 'a casus belli would not be difficult to find'. During the next few years he was to expand his ideas along these lines both in Britain and abroad.

At times he wished to keep his views private; at others he publicized them. Thus in May 1948 he did not want it to be known that he had discussed with a correspondent the destruction of a war with Russia and had then added:

> Even at such a price, I think war would be worth while. Communism must be wiped out, and world government must be established. But if, by waiting, we could defend our present lines in Germany and Italy, it would be an immeasurable boon. I do not think the Russians will yield without war. I think all (including Stalin) are fatuous and ignorant. But I hope I am wrong about this.

Yet less than a month later he was publicly writing in the *Dagens Nyheter* about Russia's probable refusal to allow inspection of nuclear plants by international officials and adding: 'Even were a precarious peace preserved for a time, one must – recalling the earlier history of human folly – expect that sooner or later war would break out. If it did, we should have a truly great cause to fight for: that of world government. . . .' Any equivocations about what he did or did not say were cleared up when in March 1959 he was interviewed on the BBC by John Freeman and was asked: 'Is it true or untrue that in recent years you advocated that a preventive war might be made against communism, against Soviet Russia?' His reply – 'It's entirely true, and I don't repent of it' – was qualified in the same interview by the contradictory comment that he had not advocated nuclear war and

Russell (centre) about to be interviewed by John Freeman (left) for the BBC 'Face to Face' programme on 4 March 1959. Hugh Burnett, producer, on right.

then further qualified by the statement that if the Russians had not given way he would have been prepared to face the consequences of using nuclear weapons against them.

Russell's belief that Russia should be constrained while time remained – and, if necessary, attacked – was the logical result of an outlook which, as revealed in his 1915 essay 'The Ethics of War', could contemplate justifiable wars. Against Russia it would, presumably, have been one of principle, since he was to write in 1950: 'The next war, if it comes, will be the greatest disaster that will have befallen the human race up to that moment. I can think of only one greater disaster: the extension of the Kremlin's power over the whole world.' This was a catastrophe which, up to the Russian acquisition of nuclear weapons in 1949, many men felt might be avoided by taking the strongest possible lead. In 1947 even Britain's Labour leaders, already preparing Britain's own nuclear weapons without the knowledge of the British public or the American government, can hardly have been too shocked at Russell's views.

In addition to his q.e.d. argument – 'as simple and as unescapable as a mathematical demonstration', as he was to claim in the *New Commonwealth* of January 1948 – there may well have been an emotional factor involved. Colette had left England in the autumn of 1939, idealistically determined to help Finland in the fight against Russian invaders. From the, admittedly scanty, evidence, it appears that her feelings were similar to Russell's. In 1941 she had moved to Sweden, returning to Britain soon after the end of the war. Russell had kept up correspondence with her, and if doubts ever arose about the logic of thwarting Russia's imperialist aims, they will have been quickly dispersed.

Russell's acceptability to those in authority reached its zenith with the Reith lectures in 1948 and the Order of Merit in the following year. In 1950 he visited Australia at the invitation of the Australian Institute of International Affairs and at the age of 78 was shuttled from one side of the continent to the other for a two-month lecture tour that would have taxed the physical and intellectual stamina of any man. He was back in Britain only a few weeks, then left for what had been planned as a single course of lectures on philosophy at Mount Holyoke College for Women in New England. Before he returned he had given the Matchette Foundation lectures at Columbia University, and agreed to return to America for what was to be a successful and more ambitious lecture tour the following year.

However, by 1951 Russell's views on international affairs, which had opened the doors to places where convicted pacifists were rarely seen, were already changing. In the summer of 1949 the Russians exploded their first nuclear weapon, thereby not only changing the balance of world power but making logically untenable the position which Russell had held for the previous four years. It would not be possible for a nation of 55 million crammed into 90,000 square miles to fight a war with nuclear-armed enemies and have any hope of survival; threatening the Russians was a policy of the past. Therefore, for Britain more than for most countries, the new task was that of ensuring that war with Russia did not break out. And therefore, almost inevitably, Russell would have to part company with those who still clung to the post-war hope that Russia could be contained by threats.

The first indication that he was about to leave one political world for another came in 1950. He had been awarded the Nobel Prize for Literature and chose as the subject of his Nobel Lecture, 'What Desires are Politically Important?' The audience in Stockholm, which included the Swedish Royal family – 'immediately put at their ease by Russell', according to one observer – heard something different from the normal technical discourse or literary exposition. Instead, they listened to an impassioned plea for peace. 'The atom bomb and the

Russell being given the Nobel Prize for Literature in 1950 by the King of Sweden, Gustaf VI Adolf. It was awarded for 'philosophical works . . . of service to moral civilization'. To a suggestion that an additional lecture or two in Sweden might boost the sale of his books in Scandinavia, Russell replied: 'I have had my fill of lecturing recently and one of the advantages of the Prize is that it will enable me to do less of it.'

bacterial bomb', they were told, 'wielded by the wicked communist or the wicked capitalist as the case may be, makes Washington and the Kremlin tremble, and drives men further and further along the road to the abyss.' Two years previously he had written: 'Communism must be wiped out and world government must be established'; but now, he admitted, one of the great dangers was 'the desire for the victory of our own ideology and the defeat of the other'.

Throughout the next four years his view that 'we cannot defeat Russia without defeating ourselves' was strengthened as the Russians began to deploy nuclear-tipped missiles targeted on western Europe and both America and the Soviet Union kept almost level-pegging in their attempts to perfect a transportable hydrogen bomb. American success in this enterprise during the spring of 1954 was probably the decisive factor in determining how Russell should spend the rest of his life.

The US hydrogen bomb test at Bikini finally confirmed what many scientists had long feared: that the dangers of radioactive fall-out were potentially even greater than expected. Russell therefore decided to preach a simple gospel: that nuclear weapons no longer offered any hope of national victory and that in the case of Britain their possession decreased rather than increased her chance of survival. His first opportunity for proclaiming this to a large audience came after he had written to the British Broadcasting Corporation in June 1954. 'In common with everybody else', he said, 'I am deeply troubled about the prospects for mankind in view of the H-bomb. I have a profound desire to do whatever lies in my power to awake people to the gravity of the issue.' Might he, Russell suggested, broadcast the final chapter of his book *Human Society in Ethics and Politics*, adding to it if necessary?

The outcome, after various other proposals had been discussed, was 'Man's Peril', an extraordinarily successful broadcast, made on 23 December, during the peak listening time which followed the nine o'clock news. In his closing words Russell starkly presented the alternatives as he summed up for his listeners: '. . . remember your humanity and forget the rest. If you can do so, the way lies open to a new Paradise; if you cannot, nothing lies before you but universal death.' 'Man's Peril' made its impact partly because of Russell's obvious sincerity and authority. Yet he used all the tricks of the trade gleaned during a lifetime of speaking; thus he quoted in support of his warning neither pacifists nor left-wingers, but rather Lord Adrian, Master of Trinity and President of the Royal Society and, a clever touch, Marshal of the Royal Air Force Sir John Slessor and Air Chief Marshal Sir Philip Joubert. A further stroke of genius, especially when addressed to a British audience, was the statement that in a nuclear war it would not only be the humans who would perish; in addition there would perish the animals, 'whom no one can accuse of Communism or anti-Communism'.

'Man's Peril' was a turning-point in Russell's life. It led to his foundation, with Albert Einstein, of the Pugwash Movement which

Albert Einstein, who – with Russell and six other Nobel Prize Winners – signed the Russell-Einstein Manifesto outlining the dangers of nuclear war. Publication of the Manifesto led to the foundation of the Pugwash Movement.

Opposite: Russell with his fourth wife, Edith, at an anti-nuclear demonstration in Trafalgar Square organized by the Campaign for Nuclear Disarmament, of which Russell was the first President.

still flourishes today. This in turn made him the natural choice as President of the Campaign for Nuclear Disarmament when it was founded in 1958, and his work in CND led almost inexorably to the Committee of 100 and his imprisonment for civil disobedience. Much of the rest now looks inevitable, given a man of Russell's uncompromising beliefs and his determination to follow the logical path whatever the consequences. Thus the Bertrand Russell Peace Foundation and the War Crimes Tribunal, ineffective and disastrous as many believe them to have been, respectively, were the results of his determination to save the world in spite of itself. Three-quarters of a century after Lady Russell had quoted her favourite text – 'Thou shalt not follow a multitude to do evil' – the legacy of Pembroke Lodge was still strong.

Russell was ideally qualified to handle the response to 'Man's Peril'. The natural assumption that he could negotiate with anyone, on equal terms, was epitomized by his meeting with Jawaharlal Nehru, the Indian Prime Minister who was passing through London early in 1955. The Indians, Nehru said, were 'prepared to do something' about the nuclear problem, an attitude apparently changed by Dr Bahba, India's leading physicist whom Russell failed to convince. Russell wrote to Einstein. Joliot-Curie, President of the influential World Federation of Scientific Workers, wrote to Russell. The outcome was the Russell-Einstein Manifesto, signed by eight other prominent scientists, six of them Nobel Prize-winners, calling for the resolution of international disputes by peaceful means since in the nuclear age the word 'victory' no longer had real meaning.

Announced in the summer of 1955, the Manifesto called for a meeting of scientists from both sides of the Iron Curtain. It took place when twenty-two men assembled in 1957 at Pugwash, Nova Scotia, the home of Cyrus Eaton, the Canadian financier who funded the meeting. Russell himself attended only two of the Pugwash Conferences which from now on were held regularly at different centres throughout the world. His importance lay elsewhere, mainly in convincing potential supporters that the Movement was not part of a Russian-financed plot. This was far from being the case; Russell himself adopted the 'plague on both your houses' attitude. He maintained that unilateral disarmament was useless and as late as September 1957 was writing in *The New York Times*: 'America has become the torch-bearer for the West, and it is the duty of all of us to do what we can to keep the torch burning brightly.' Until the Vietnam War introduced a new factor on to the international scene, Russell's argument was the simple, and in many places unpopular, advocacy of mutual disarmament and of lessening tension between the two super-powers.

The British hydrogen bomb and the rise of the Campaign for Nuclear Disarmament altered all that. There had been protest movements before CND – the Hydrogen Bomb National Committee, the Emergency Committee for Direct Action and the Council for the

Russell with Cyrus Eaton, the
Canadian millionaire after whose
hometown the Pugwash
Movement was named. Both had
just addressed the final session of
the third Pugwash Conference at
the Akademie der Wissenschaften
in Vienna on Saturday, 20
September 1958.

Abolition of Nuclear Weapon Tests among others. None made more
than a minimal impact in Britain and it was left to CND to attract a
national following and, in the autumn of 1960, to come within an ace
of committing the Labour Party to renunciation of nuclear weapons.

The Campaign had been founded by such well-known figures as
J. B. Priestley (the novelist), Victor Gollancz (the publisher),
Kingsley Martin (editor of *The New Statesman*), and Canon Collins (of
St Paul's). But influential as all of them were, they needed someone
who could be both a rallying-point and a symbol. Who better than
Russell, with his televisually perfect mane of white hair, his stern
principles and lucid prose, the philosopher who with his 'Man's Peril'
seemed genuinely to have awakened in many countries at least a
tentative realization of what nuclear war would mean? So Russell,

now in his eighty-sixth year, entered the world of protest meetings and sit-downs on wet pavements that could look ridiculous or heroic according to point of view, and of vilification by much of the press which suggested that things had not changed a lot since the First World War.

Whether Russell played a bigger part in the Campaign's failures than in its successes is even now not easy to assess. Despite his foundation of the break-away Committee of 100 which split the movement down the middle, his impressive figure, his cogent arguments, and his ability to deal with hecklers as if they were recalcitrant undergraduates deliberately failing to listen, gave a panache to CND that it would otherwise have lacked. The reverse side of the coin has been described by A. J. P. Taylor, himself a leading member of CND:

> Like any President of a Society, he was meant to be a figurehead – not to come to executive meetings, not to lay down policy, but just to give us his benign blessing and there his name would be at the top of the letter paper. But instead of that he thought he was much better fitted to run the Campaign for Nuclear Disarmament than we were. I thought he was a frightful nuisance.

Russell's interventions would have been even more numerous had changes in his private life not brought him by the later 1950s to the remoteness of North Wales. While still in Cambridge it had become clear that his third marriage was breaking up. First he moved to Richmond on the outskirts of the capital. Peter divorced him for desertion, apparently under the impression that he wished to marry Colette, a reasonable impression since Colette had been staying with him in North Wales and was preparing to buy a cottage there. However, once the decree absolute was signed Russell married Edith Finch, the friend of Lucy Donnelly he had met in Princeton a decade earlier. Colette, in hospital and expecting to go blind from glaucoma, heard the news from a newspaper. 'Fortunately the glaucoma proved a scare', she wrote. 'But that day was one of the worst in my life.'

Russell's fourth wife was some thirty years his junior, dedicated both to him and to the liberal causes he supported. A more than competent organizer, both attractive and witty, she was ideally suited to be the companion of his last eighteen years. With her he moved, as it were, from the centre of the battle to a vantage-point from which he could objectively survey the scene, to Plas Penrhyn, a Regency house on the Portmeirion Peninsula. It provided him not only with solitude but with an incomparable panorama of the Glaslyn estuary and the horseshoe peaks of the Snowdon massif, as well as a glimpse of Tan-y-Rallt where Shelley was attacked after being sent down from Oxford. A new flat in London was acquired for the rare visits south, but it was from Plas Penrhyn that he sallied out to speak at CND meetings throughout the country, and to broadcast; and it was mainly in Plas Penrhyn that he continued to write articles that had only one message but were trimmed and tailored for the most contrasting of publications.

Russell with his fourth wife, Edith Finch, at the time of their marriage on 15 December 1952.

Russell's third wife, Peter (right), after she had been granted a divorce on the grounds of desertion in June 1952.

Above. Plas Penrhyn, the small Regency house on the Portmeirion peninsula in north Wales to which Russell and his wife moved in 1955. *Left:* The view from his bedroom. In the foreground lies the Glaslyn estuary, while in the distance there are the horseshoe of the Snowdon peaks; the Moelwyns; and the unlikely and dramatic peak of Cnicht, 'the Matterhorn of North Wales'. *Opposite:* At his desk. Although in his mid-80s when he moved to his new home, he continued to write vigorously and prolifically.

In support of CND, Russell wrote for Canada's *International Affairs* and for the Indian *Radical Humanist*. But he was equally at home writing 'Four Minute Madness' for the *Sunday Dispatch* and giving the message to *Maclean's Magazine* and *John Bull*. For scientists and philosophers who wrote only for the élite and the specialists, he must have been a constant irritant. Articles and addresses to public meetings were only two of the weapons he used in an effort to bring people to their senses, and in the much-despised House of Lords he organized a motion urging Britain to persuade the non-nuclear powers to renounce the manufacture, ownership and use of nuclear weapons. Despite support from Lord Adrian and the Bishops of Manchester, Portsmouth and Chichester, the motion was, by leave, withdrawn. 'Nobody', observed Russell four years later, 'takes the House of Lords seriously, and there is no particular reason why anyone should.'

In 1960 he changed his stance in a move reminiscent of 1915. Then, he had decided that his opposition to the war had been insufficient and had dedicated himself to the No-Conscription Fellowship, eager for martyrdom. Now, equally realistic, he felt that CND had shot its bolt and that something more effective was needed for success. The result was the Committee of 100, first proposed by his young recruit, Ralph Schoenman, but a potential force which Russell believed might satisfy what he saw as the demands of the situation.

Schoenman was a young American studying at the London School of Economics. He had been involved in the protest movement for the previous few years, and in July 1960 wrote to Russell, asking for help in organizing a demonstration of civil disobedience. He then hitch-hiked to Penrhyndeudraeth, charmed both Russell and his wife, and by 11 September had helped Russell draft letters announcing that a group of 100 people called 'The Committee of 100 for Civil Disobedience against Nuclear Warfare' was being formed. Like so many other operations of the Committee of 100, the announcement of the new group appears to have been bungled, although Russell's later statement that a policy of civil disobedience had been chosen 'purely to get attention' suggests that the bungling may have been intended. After some days of cantankerous dispute between the leaders of the old Campaign and of the new Committee – in which a tape-recorder was used to ensure that neither side misquoted the other – Russell resigned from the Presidency of the CND.

Schoenman, frequently operating from London where he began to speak as the voice of the Master, now became his personal secretary. From the autumn of 1960 until the summer of 1969, when Russell broke his last links with Schoenman, each man used the other with varying success. The claims that Schoenman, the brash American, dominated a senile Russell do not bear inspection. More accurately, it can be said that for the first few years of the 1960s Russell was glad to use the services of a young man with ideas quite as radical as his own and an audacious ability to get things done. Only slowly did he realize

Russell addressing Edinburgh members of the Campaign for Nuclear Disarmament in Trafalgar Square after they had arrived in London on 24 September 1960 headed by the Arliston Colliery Pipe Band. Russell was 88 at the time. *Left:* Russell at a nuclear demonstration, seen with Ralph Schoenman (bottom right), the controversial young American who became his secretary in 1960 and who was largely responsible for the birth of the Committee of 100.

BERTRAND RUSSELL SWIMS ATLANTIC

In an amazing feat unparalleled in the history of the world Bertrand Russell the 94 year old philosopher and "Happy Pilgrim of Peace" yesterday swam the Atlantic Ocean in two hours.

The news was revealed in a special dispatch from the Ralph Schoenman Press Bureau, at Penrhyndendraeth, Merionethshire.

FANTASTIC

According to the dispatch, Earl Russell ("our respected and beloved leader")entered the chilly waters of the Atlantic Sea at 6.00 p.m. yesterday morning.

"The Atlantic" says the report "was raging in a violent tempest of wind and rain. Giant waves, many of them a million feet high, crashed in anger on the rocky coast."

INCREDIBLE

But Lord Russell was not to be deterred by the elements. "Looking ruddy and cheerful, his muscles shining with youthful vigour, he leapt into the swirling waters and within minutes was well out to sea."

With him were the local secretary of The Committee of 100, the Organising Chairman of Bombs for the Viet Cong (Wales) Association and Mr. Schoenman himself.

MIRACLE

"As Earl Russell breasted the mighty billows of the deep" the report continues, "he chatted jokingly with his companions only pausing to kill marauding sharks with a savage blow from his virile fist or tear of slabs of whalemeat to relieve the hunger of his comrades."

Within two hours the party had landed in America and were taking part in a sit-down demonstration outside the White House.

ASTONISHING

Reporters were not allowed to witness the actual swimming but later photographs were issued (one of which we reprint above). "These" the report states, "will put paid to the lying and slanderous smears on the part of the capitalist lackeys and hacks of the warmongering British Press as to the alleged senility or even death of the righteous warrior of peace."

that the audacity was frequently counter-productive and that his own standing was being steadily eroded. *Private Eye*'s news story headed 'Bertrand Russell Swims Atlantic' caught exactly the air of thoughtless claim that was sometimes created in London on behalf of Russell in Penrhyndeudraeth.

He himself was capable of serious misjudgments, even without Schoenman's intervention. Thus success and failure alternated during the last ten years of his life, during which he campaigned against nuclear weapons, intervened in the Cuban crisis of 1962, protested against American intervention in Vietnam and let his still considerable energies loose on a variety of causes that included the Arab-Israeli confrontation, the Sino-Indian dispute, and a War Crimes Tribunal set up to accuse one side in the Vietnam War.

Despite his creation of the Committee of 100, Russell continued to support, and to speak for, the Campaign for Nuclear Disarmament. At times his intervention was inept, as when at Birmingham in April 1961 he maintained that Kennedy and Macmillan were 'much more wicked than Hitler'. The damage caused by such statements was balanced later in the year when Russell and his wife were summoned to appear at Bow Street magistrate's court to answer a charge, made under an act of 1361, of inciting the public to civil disobedience. Few

Russell and his wife leaving Bow Street Court on 12 September 1961 after being sentenced to two months in prison under an act of 1361 for inciting the public to civil disobedience. The sentences were reduced to a week, and were both served in prison hospitals – where Russell read a number of detective stories and the life of Madame de Staël.

Opposite: An item from the satirical *Private Eye*, published on 15 August 1966, which reflected the exaggerated statements sometimes made on Russell's behalf.

things could have pleased Russell more. 'We instructed [our barrister]', he later said, 'to try to prevent our being let off scot-free, but, equally, to try to have us sentenced to not longer than a fortnight in prison.'

All went as Russell had hoped. He made a brief but telling speech from the dock, and while the sentence on both defendants was of two months, this was reduced to one week and was served in prison hospitals. As *The New Statesman* commented, the authorities had 'behaved with a unique, one might say almost inspired, blend of stupidity and panic'. A man in his ninetieth year, sentenced to prison for what he obviously believed to be right, could not fail to win the respect of many who strongly disagreed with his opinions. Almost overnight, the public image of the ancient philosopher sitting on public pavements to no purpose was transformed into that of the noble eccentric.

The propaganda benefits of this second imprisonment in a long life were still in existence when, almost exactly a year later, Russell intervened in the Cuban crisis which threatened to bring America and Russia to the brink of nuclear war. As an American blockade of the island appeared imminent a statement was issued to the press from Plas Penrhyn. As typed it began, 'Mankind is faced tonight with a grave crisis.' This was altered in Schoenman's hand to: 'It seems likely that within a week you will all be dead to please American madmen.' On Russell's suggestion, 'a week' was altered to 'a week or two', but otherwise the statement was issued as Schoenman had altered it. When the blockade was announced a few hours later Russell despatched five cables from Plas Penrhyn. President Kennedy; Premier Krushchev; U-Thant, Secretary-General of the United Nations; Harold Macmillan, the British Prime Minister, and Hugh Gaitskell, leader of the British Opposition, were all appealed to in various ways, with the cables to Kennedy and U Thant strongly condemning the American action.

So far, events had not been particularly remarkable since Russell was regularly writing to, or cabling, heads of State with a near-familiarity which might have been effective in the days of Lord John but appeared to have little impact in the second half of the twentieth century. Then, within forty-eight hours of Russell's cables, Moscow Radio began broadcasting a reply to Russell from Premier Krushchev, an event which brought Russell nearer to the centre of the scene. Press and radio correspondents immediately made for Penrhyndeudraeth to interview the 'nonagenarian intellectual in carpet slippers in his cottage in North Wales'.

During the next three days Russell sent further cables to Kennedy and Krushchev as well as to Castro. Eventually the Russians agreed to withdraw from Cuba the missiles which had been the cause of the confrontation, but there is no evidence to suggest that Russell's intervention affected the course of events. There had been exchanges between Krushchev and Kennedy of which Russell knew nothing and he himself later said: 'I do not consider that I have altered the course

Russell preparing on 9 April 1960 for a transatlantic exchange with Edward Teller, 'the father of the H-bomb'. Nuclear tests and freedom of speech were some of the subjects discussed.

of history by one hair's-breadth.' To Lord Dundee at the Foreign Office he confided: 'Probably Krushchev only does what I ask if he has decided to do it anyhow.'

The exaggerated claims made by Russell's supporters for his influence on the Cuban crisis did much to qualify his credibility during the following years. However, those few weeks in the autumn of 1962 had shown Russell that his self-imposed task of saving the world from destruction needed a great deal of money. His ability to earn high fees by writing or speaking was now being limited by age and, in any case, money of a new order of magnitude was necessary. Undeterred, he embarked on a three-point plan that was to be remarkably successful.

First, he set up the Bertrand Russell Peace Foundation and the Atlantic Foundation and appealed for money to run them. Secondly,

he decided to publish his autobiography which he knew would produce a considerable sum. Thirdly, he offered to the highest bidder the huge collection of papers, letters and manuscripts which he had accumulated since his youth. Together, the receipts enabled him to fund a major programme of political activity.

During these final years Russell took up the cause of political prisoners in Brazil, Burma, the Congo, Greece, the Philippines and Iraq. But he also appealed on behalf of political prisoners in Russia and he protested as strongly as any irate Conservative politician against Russia's testing of ever more destructive nuclear weapons. This is so frequently overlooked, Russell's alleged pro-Communism so frequently constructed out of myth, that too much emphasis cannot be put on it. His unwillingness, as he put it, 'to give in to the Russian usage according to which the word "democratic" means a military tyranny imposed by alien forces – as in East Germany and Hungary', lasted until death.

During the 1960s Russell's fears of nuclear disaster tended to be overshadowed by the war in Vietnam. One reason was probably his belief that as both sides had drawn back from the brink during the Cuban crisis, the prospect of nuclear war had diminished; if this were so, Vietnam should, for the time being, take priority. He had suspected American statements about Vietnam long before most people in Britain were prepared to do so. Many of his suspicions were later found to be justified and it is curious that his book, *War Crimes in Vietnam*, and the work of the War Crimes Tribunal which he set up, should have been so counter-productive. One reason was no doubt the strength of his horror and the knowledge that, in his nineties, he had no time to waste. So in the book he abandoned the calculated rapier-like attack that had served him so well for so long; instead, he slashed about with the intensity – and the vulnerability – of a man wielding a broadsword he could not fully control.

From the War Crimes Tribunal onwards, his reliance on Ralph Schoenman diminished more quickly. Although the final breach did not come until the summer of 1969, he had long before this begun to rely on a corps of other young men who ran the Peace Foundation and translated his beliefs into action. His inner toughness, the outcome of inheritance and Pembroke Lodge, still enabled him even at 97 to keep at bay most of the illnesses of old age. At times, large doses of antibiotics were needed and for a day or so he would be both mentally and physically off-colour. He snapped back quickly enough, and it was an alert Russell who on the afternoon of 31 January 1970 dictated to his secretary, Christopher Farley, a message to be read to the International Conference of Parliamentarians in Cairo. Vintage Russell, it condemned Israel for bombing Egypt and noted that 'to invoke the horrors of the past to justify those of the present is gross hypocrisy'.

Two days afterwards, he felt rather ill in the early evening and retired to his bed. An hour later he was dead.

Russell with the Pears Trophy awarded in 1955 in recognition of his work for world peace.

On the hills of Snowdonia. 'I remember him reaching the top of Cnicht when he was 77 and I was 11 and our climbing powers were approximately equal', his younger son Conrad has said, 'and I remember him at 95, swinging over the steps to the balcony for the sheer delight of the view of Snowdon in the afternoon sun.'

Russell had in many ways been typical of the vigorous Victorians, radiating what appeared to be limitless energy, defending his beliefs with resolute lack of compromise but willing to change those beliefs if reason seemed to demand a change. Perhaps his greatest weakness was his faith that reason would always conquer if only the facts were explained simply enough. It was therefore natural that his greatest achievements should be in the stratosphere of mathematics and logic where human feelings were of no account. Equally natural was his failure to enjoy, until old age, anything more than a life perpetually fraught with personal worry.

If his first real love had been mathematics, his next had been Trinity, and he would have approved the memorial inscription put there after his death. It read, in translation from the Latin:

> The third Earl Russell, O.M., Fellow of this College, was particularly famous as a writer on, and interpreter of, Mathematical Logic. Long appalled at human bitterness, as an old man – but with the verve of youth – he devoted himself entirely to the preservation of peace among nations, until finally, the recipient of numerous honours and a man respected throughout the world, he found rest from his labours in 1970, in his 98th year.

The memorial inscription in
Trinity College Chapel,
Cambridge.

BERTRAND RUSSELL
Comes Russell tertius, O.M., huius Collegii socius,
philosophiae praesertim mathematicae scriptor
et interpres inclaruit. Idem, amentiam hominum
diu indignatus, senex iuuenili impetu paci inter
gentes seruandae totus incubuit donec tandem
multis adfectus honoribus et per orbem terrarum
obseruatus anno aetatis suae XCVIII, salutis MCMLXX,
e laboribus conquieuit.

SELECT BIBLIOGRAPHY

The place of publication is London unless otherwise stated

Ronald W. Clark, *The Life of Bertrand Russell* (1975)

Rupert Crawshay-Williams, *Russell Remembered* (1970)

J. Dewey and H. M. Kallen (eds), *The Bertrand Russell Case* (New York 1941)

Robert Gathorne-Hardy, *Ottoline at Garsington* (1974)

G. H. Hardy, *Bertrand Russell and Trinity* (1970)

Jean van Heijenoort, *From Frege to Gödel: A Source Book in Mathematical Logic, 1879–1931* (Cambridge, Mass., 1967)

Georg Kreisel, 'Bertrand Russell, F.R.S.', *Biographical Memoirs of Fellows of the Royal Society* (vol. 19, 1973, 583–620)

Victor Lowe, *Understanding Whitehead* (Johns Hopkins University Press, Baltimore, Md., 1966)

Harry T. Moore (ed), *D. H. Lawrence's Letters to Bertrand Russell* (New York 1948)

R. A. Parker, *The Transatlantic Smiths* (New York 1960)

Russell: The Journal of the Bertrand Russell Archives (Hamilton, Ontario, Spring 1971–)

PRINCIPAL WORKS OF BERTRAND RUSSELL

The Principles of Mathematics (1903)

Principia Mathematica (with A. N. Whitehead) (1910–13)

Philosophical Essays (1910)

The Problems of Philosophy (1912)

Our Knowledge of the External World (1914)

Principles of Social Reconstruction (1916)

Mysticism and Logic (1918)

Introduction to Mathematical Philosophy (1919)

The Practice and Theory of Bolshevism (1920)

The Analysis of Mind (1921)

The Problem of China (1922)

Selected Papers of Bertrand Russell (New York 1927)

The Analysis of Matter (1927)

Marriage and Morals (1929)

Religion and Science (1935)

The Amberley Papers (with Patricia Russell) (2 vols, 1937)

An Inquiry into Meaning and Truth (New York 1940)

A History of Western Philosophy (New York 1945)

Human Knowledge: Its Scope and Limits (1948)

Authority and the Individual (1949)

Portraits from Memory (1956)

My Philosophical Development (1959)

The Basic Writings of Bertrand Russell (ed L. E. Dennon and R. E. Egner, 1961)

The Autobiography of Bertrand Russell (3 vols, 1967, 1968 and 1969)

CHRONOLOGY

1872 18 May, born Ravenscroft, Trelleck, Monmouthshire

1874 Death of mother and infant sister

1876 Death of father. Taken to live with grandparents, Lord and Lady Russell, at Pembroke Lodge, Richmond Park

1889 Wins mathematical scholarship to Cambridge

1890 Enters Trinity College, Cambridge

1893 Obtains first-class degree in mathematics

1894 Obtains first class in Moral Science examinations. Appointed attaché at British Embassy in Paris. Marries Alys Pearsall Smith

1895 Wins Fellowship at Trinity with dissertation on 'The Foundations of Geometry'

1896 Lectures at London School of Economics. Visits USA. Lectures on non-Euclidean geometry at Bryn Mawr College and Johns Hopkins University

1907 Unsuccessfully stands for Parliament in Wimbledon by-election

1908 Elected Fellow of the Royal Society

1910 Appointed Lecturer in Logic and Principles of Mathematics at Trinity College

1911 Liaison with Lady Ottoline Morrell. Leaves wife

1914 Second trip to USA. Delivers Lowell Lectures at Harvard

1916 Delivers in London course of public lectures on *Principles of Social Reconstruction*. Active with No-Conscription Fellowship. Open letter to President Wilson. Writes on behalf of imprisoned conscientious objector; is prosecuted and fined £100. Dismissed from lectureship at Trinity

1918 Imprisoned for six months for article in *The Tribunal*. Delivers public lectures on *The Philosophy of Logical Atomism*

1920 Visits Soviet Union with Labour delegation. Has interview with Lenin. Visits China with his future wife, Dora Black

1921 Lectures at National University of Peking. Divorce from Alys. Marries Dora Black. Birth of son John Conrad

1922 Unsuccessfully stands for Parliament in Chelsea as Labour candidate

1923 Birth of daughter Katharine Jane

1924 Lecture tour in USA

1927 With his wife starts experimental school at Telegraph House, Petersfield. Lecture tour in USA

1929 Lecture tour in USA

1931 Lecture tour in USA. Becomes 3rd Earl Russell on death of brother

1935 Divorce from Dora

1936 Marriage to Patricia Spence

1937 Birth of second son Conrad Sebastian Robert

1938 Appointed Visiting Professor of Philosophy at University of Chicago

1939 Appointed Professor of Philosophy at University of California at Los Angeles

1940 Offered professorship at New York City College. Appointment revoked following controversial court case

1941–3 Lectures at Barnes Foundation, Merion, Pennsylvania, on the history of philosophy

1944 Appointed Fellow of Trinity College; returns to England

1948 Many broadcasts for the BBC. Sent to Norway by British Council

1949 Delivers first Reith Lectures on BBC. Member of the Order of Merit

1950 Travels to Australia and USA as visiting lecturer. Awarded Nobel Prize for Literature

1952 Divorce from Patricia. Marriage to Edith Finch

1954 'Man's Peril' broadcast on BBC

1957 Elected President of first Pugwash Conference. Publication of his Open Letter to Krushchev and Eisenhower urging cooperation between East and West

1958 Helps found Campaign for Nuclear Disarmament

1960 Resigns from Presidency of CND. Becomes President of the Committee of 100

1961 Protests against British Government's nuclear policies. With Lady Russell sentenced to two months' imprisonment, reduced to one week for reasons of health

1963 Launches Bertrand Russell Peace Foundation

1970 Death on 2 February

LIST OF ILLUSTRATIONS

Numbers refer to page numbers

INDEX